Endorsements

Nick Gough has written a timely book that encourages the church to live a both/and message rather than an either/or. He captures the heart of being a people of the Word and the Spirit, resulting in love that can change the world!
— Tammy Donahoo, Vice-President of U.S. Operations, General Supervisor; The Foursquare Church

The Bible is clear that our witness of Jesus must be accompanied by supernatural power (Acts 1:8). In his book, When the Old Becomes New, author Nick Gough presents both a clear theology and a practical methodology for how every believer can become an empowered witness of Jesus. This book contains an incredible amount of biblical truth, historical accounts, experiential wisdom, and practical steps for those who are ready to live out the pages of the Bible in the world today. I encourage everyone to read it, apply it, and share it with others to Ignite a hunger for more as we follow Jesus!
— Ben Dixon, Director, Ignite Global Ministries; author of *Hearing God* and *Prophesy.*

WHEN THE
OLD BECOMES NEW

You are
a world
changer!

Nick

──── WHEN THE ────

OLD BECOMES NEW

*Embracing the Gifts of the Spirit
to Change A Culture*

DR. NICK GOUGH

eGenCo

eGenCo
824 Tallow Hill Road
Chambersburg, PA 17202, USA
Phone: 717-461-3436
Email: info@egen.co
Website: www.egen.co

 facebook.com/egenbooks

 youtube.com/egenpub

 egen.co/blog

 pinterest.com/eGenDMP

 twitter.com/egen_co

 instagram.com/egen.co

Publisher's Cataloging-in-Publication Data

Gough, Nick
When the Old Becomes New. Embracing the Gifts of the Spirit
to Change a Culture.; by Nick Gough. Stephen Nance, editor.
200 pages cm.
ISBN: 978-1-68019-001-4 Paperback
       978-1-68019-002-1 ebook
       978-1-68019-003-8 ebook

1. Religion. 2. Holy Spirit. 3. Christian Worldview. I. Title

2019938800

To my loving wife, Robin, and our five daughters, who have been so amazingly supportive and encouraging to me in my walk with Jesus. To all my friends in the ministry who have been chasing after the move of God, you inspire me to go deeper with the Lord.

Table of Contents

Chapter One

What Changed My Life

I hate how easy it is for people to become "champions" of spiritual formation without actually becoming transformed...I hate how hard spiritual transformation is and how long it takes. I hate thinking about how many people have gone to church for decades and remain joyless or judgmental or bitter or superior.

– John Ortberg[1]

How many Christians do you know today who seem bitter, joyless, powerless, and judgmental (at least, most of the time)? Rather than we transforming our culture today, our culture is transforming us. What would our society look like if we, as the church, collectively started to act like the Book of Acts? Transforming a culture that doesn't know God?

This book will give you tools to become a soul winner and miracle worker. But before we begin, I think it is important that you know what transformed my life from a nominal skeptical seeker of Christ to a sold-out disciple of Christ.

I have been in ministry for over 35 years, but it was an encounter with the power of God as a teenager that brought the gospel from head knowledge to heart knowledge for me. Southern California during the 60s and 70s, as in much of the rest of the nation, was a tumultuous time: the Vietnam War; the Civil Rights movement; the assassinations of President John F. Kennedy and Dr. Martin Luther King, Jr.; college campus antiwar protests; strong popular discontent

1

with the government. Social unrest permeated the culture, and in the midst of it all the Jesus Movement began bubbling up.

Having grown up in church, I knew all the stories—Noah's Ark, David and Goliath, Moses parting the Red Sea, etc.—but they had little effect on me. They were neat stories, but that's all they were—stories from long ago that were not personally relevant to me. As far as I was concerned, the Bible accounts, especially those involving miracles, detailed events that had happened to a group of guys way back in the first century. But those kinds of events didn't happen today; at least, that is what I was told. I had never experienced anything remotely like a miracle, healing, or any move of the Holy Spirit that seemed to be so normative in the New Testament. Consequently, I thought of Christianity as a bunch of stories that had no basis in today's reality. The early followers of Christ might have done and experienced all those things, but not today. That was my paradigm of Christianity.

This book is for those who think there has got to be more to Christianity than just a collection of old stories; that being a Christian is more than just knowing—or even believing—those stories; that maybe there really is a God who wants to intervene in our lives and use us to do the same kind of stuff that we read so clearly in the New Testament accounts.

So, how did the Bible change my life? My junior year in high school was a tumultuous time for me. One of my friends was going through a very bad case of barbiturate withdrawals. It was a Saturday night in 1976, and we had heard about something unusual that was happening in Costa Mesa, California at Chuck Smith's church, Calvary Chapel. They actually had rock bands playing Christian music! This was totally revolutionary for the church at that time, a development that many looked down on as not being from God. Many traditional churches were aghast: "You mean they actually have drums and electric guitars in church?"

A band called Mustard Seed Faith was playing that night at Calvary Chapel, so we hopped into my friend's VW Bug and started the drive down south. When we got to Calvary Chapel, there was a long line of people waiting to go in. My friend was starting to lose it, so we decided to sit down on the back wall so no one would notice us. Tom Stipes, the hosting pastor of Calvary Chapel, Costa Mesa, that night said from the pulpit, "There is a guy out there who is going through drug withdrawals and the Lord is going to heal him." Now there must have been over a thousand people there that night, and we were sure he couldn't see us. Even if he could, how would he know this?

As soon as my friend heard those words, he changed in a moment from shaking and sweating to completely calm and peaceful. It was immediately and visibly noticeable what the Lord had done. At that time, I did not have a vocabulary for what I had seen or what Tom Stipes had done. All I knew was that my friend was healed, set free, and at peace. I remember hitting the guy next to me and saying, "Do you see this?" For lack of a better term, I could see the Holy Spirit on him; Shekinah glory, manifest presence, a distinct glow; whatever you want to call it, I saw it on him. I felt like Gomer Pyle from the Andy Griffith Show, who often said, "Shazam," whenever something astonished him.

My Christianity changed in an instant from the theoretical to the experiential; from the speculative to the genuine, authenticated, verifiable reality of Jesus doing what He said He would do in Luke 4:18, "The Spirit of the Lord is on me, because he has anointed me to proclaim good news to the poor. He has sent me to proclaim freedom for the prisoners and recovery of sight for the blind, to set the oppressed free" (NIV). My friend was healed, set free of drug addiction, and accepted Jesus without any evangelistic program, but by a miracle, all of it instantaneous. Right before my eyes, I witnessed something undeniably supernatural.

Tom Stipes later gave an altar call for all those who wanted more of Jesus. I responded right then and there. I wanted this Jesus who could heal and set people free. I wanted a powerful God who could intervene in my life, not some God who used to do miracles but stopped doing so in the first century. I wanted this real, all-powerful God who loved me and could intervene in my world.

Later that night, after dropping my friend off, I went home, walked into my room, immediately opened my Bible and began to read. Before, reading the Bible for me was like the old Peanuts cartoons where Charlie Brown's and Lucy's teacher would sound to them like "wa, wa, wa," as they started to nod off in class. Now, however, it was completely different. For the first time it was like God was speaking to me through the Bible. That night, without a theology, paradigm, or minister-led prompting, I began to speak in a language that I did not know. I began to speak in tongues. I was so excited about this experience that I told my youth pastor about what had happened. I expected him to be as happy as I was, but I was wrong. "That stuff doesn't happen today," he told me.

Needless to say, I was disillusioned. You mean to tell me that God can't do this stuff? Is He the great "I Am," or the great "I Was"? I went off to college not firmly set in my faith, not really sure if what I had experienced was real or not. If the things in the Bible can't happen today, then is the Bible real? Is it still relevant? Is God real? Is Christianity real since it is based on miracles? Christians believe in a virgin birth, in Moses parting the Red Sea, in the death, burial, and resurrection of Christ. How then could God quit doing the miraculous since it's in His very nature as the all-powerful God? Did God's nature change? Is He no longer *Jehovah Rapha*, as in Exodus 15:26, "I am the LORD, who heals you" (NIV)? He is the great "I AM," present tense; at least, that is how Moses encountered Him. He is the unchanging God who changes us, heals us, and sets us free.

During my sophomore year of my undergraduate studies at the University of Southern California, I came to a crisis in my life. I was in an environment full of people whose parents were extremely wealthy and influential. The American Dream and caught hold of me; I thought that making money was the key to success and that USC was the right environment to prepare me for it. I was in a fraternity and living the life, but I soon realized that the people that I was hanging around with were just as broken and empty as I was. If money was the idea of success, then why were all these rich kids so broken, arrogant, and lost?

Tom Sirotnik, a friend of mine who had grown up with me in Long Beach, California, played football in high school. We both ended up going to USC. Tom was the first freshman in 20 years to walk on and make the football team. He played football for USC when they were national champs in 1978. If you are a college football buff, that was the year of Marcus Allen, Ronnie Lott, Anthony Munoz, Charles White, and Chip Banks, all of whom played for USC. They would end up becoming some of the best NFL players ever to walk onto the field.

One day Tom invited me to a meeting where Rice Broocks was speaking. Rice, a powerful evangelist, is also the best-selling author of *God's Not Dead* and its sequel, *Man, Myth, Messiah*. When Rice spoke that night, I felt like God was telling me, "Do you remember who I am and what I did for you?" I couldn't resist the Lord's prompting that night, so I rededicated my life to Jesus and was baptized in a horse trough that this campus group had set up. It was then and there that I knew that the purpose of life is more than making money. Making money is not the American Dream; it is the American Myth. The purpose of life is to know Jesus Christ (John 17:3) and to make Him known (which is the subtitle of another of Rice's books, *The Human Right*). I now knew why I had been created, and that I had a destiny, a purpose in life that far exceeded the materialism of this world.

When I was 22, I became radically zealous for the Lord. The group I was with started praying for anyone and everyone on campus. We did open-air preaching at Tommy Trojan, the epicenter of USC's campus. We prayed for everyone to be healed and to come to Jesus, and we saw the Lord do this with many. One of the first miracles we witnessed at the USC was the healing of Michael Alo.

Michael Alo was a huge Samoan who had played football at Banning High School.[2] One day during a practice drill, Michael went head-to-head against Chip Banks, a future NFL Hall of Famer.[3] It was a one-on-one drill where the player who picked up the ball first, Michael in this case, had to tackle his opponent head on. Michael, who had 32-inch thighs, slammed head-on into Chip. After the collision of these two titans, Chip stood up, but Michael could not, because Chip had hit him so hard that he had snapped Michael's neck. Michael was 21 years old and destined to be a quadriplegic. We went to the hospital to pray for Michael. When we got there, it seemed as though half of Samoa was there in the hallway. We didn't know any better; we just believed that when we prayed for people, they would be healed. When we prayed for Michael, he started to say in his pidgin-English accent, "Brada, I can feel my toes. I can move my fingers!"

The doctor happened to walk into the room at that moment and asked what was going on. Michael told him that Jesus had just healed him.

"That's quite a normal reaction for quadriplegics," the doctor explained. Then he held out two fingers. "Grip these in your hand and squeeze as hard as you can."

The doctor winced in pain as this huge USC football player dealt him a crushing handshake to his fingers. It was obvious to everyone in the room that Jesus had just healed Michael. Not only could he move his fingers; he also could walk. This was the evangelistic opportunity of a life time. Michael, who moments before had been paralyzed, was now moving and walking. We called everyone in the hallway to brag on what Jesus had just done. It was kind of like what Jesus did in Matthew 4, when He healed every sick person who was brought to Him. He did it then, and I was realizing that He still does it now. I was just 22 when I saw this, and it set the course of my life.

Later that week, an evangelist named Clay McClain spoke at a campus meeting at USC. He told us that he could hear the voice of God for others. Jesus said, "My sheep listen to my voice" (Jn. 10:27a

NIV). In the New Testament, this becomes normative Christianity. Now, rather than just a few select people who could hear Him, we all can. Jesus didn't say only special people could hear Him; He said His sheep could. I had always thought that was a figurative term, not something that was a literal function of the New Testament church.

The leadership organized a prayer time for those who had just been baptized and given their hearts to Jesus. They lined everyone in a row, and Clay started to minister prophetically to the group.[4] I had never experienced anything like this before in my life. When I was called up for prayer, Clay McClain called me by name. "Your name is Nicholas Paul. Paul means 'little' and Nicholas means 'conqueror.'" I didn't have a name badge on and I had never met this man before, so this amazed me. How did he know this about me? Does God really know me? What is funny about his word to me is that I am only five-foot-eight, so yes, I do not have a gigantic stature. He went on to tell me that God had made me fast in the natural and was going to do the same in the spiritual. I used to run track and had set a lot of records in high school that still hold today, some 40 years later. I asked my friend, "How did Clay know these things? Who told him?" Prior to this, Jesus was to me just a person in a book filled with stories that a Sunday school teacher taught; He had never been a God who knew me or wanted to interact with me. This encounter with the prophetic, however, screamed loudly, "I know you and want a relationship with you!" God is interested in me and knows me? What a provocative thought, that God is a personal God. I am not some random consequence of nature; I have been purposed by God and for God (Jer.1:8).

In 1 Corinthians 14:25, Paul talks about prophecy as an evangelistic tool, or as a means for man to acknowledge that God is real. He says that when we prophesy to an unbeliever, "the secrets of his heart are disclosed; and so, he will fall on his face and worship God, declaring that God is certainly among you."

7

Clay's prophetic word to me changed my life. It moved my walk with God from theoretical knowledge to relational knowledge. I used to make fun of Christians who said, "Christianity is not a religion, but a relationship." In a relationship, we interact with one another. Prayer, at that moment, became no longer a monologue in a relationship, but a dialogue. Jesus said, "...you will know the truth, and the truth will set you free" (Jn. 8:32 NIV). Previously, my idea about knowing the truth was knowing about the Bible. It was information, and I thought that the more information I had, the more power and authority I had. This experience was different. It wasn't knowing "about"; this was a relational "knowing," something that I could know not just intellectually through reason, but personally through experience. In Psalm 34:8 David says, "O taste and see that the LORD is good." He doesn't say, "*Read* and see." He says that we can experience God in our senses. I am not implying that studying the Bible is not a way to experience God; it is, and we should be students of the Bible. Our problem is that in the church today we have made this an "either-or" scenario when it should be a "both-and" experience; the Word *and* the Spirit.

It was in these early days of ministry that I experienced many miracles associated with hearing God's voice. One such encounter was on a Tuesday evening in 1982 at USC. An intercessory prayer meeting was under way on fraternity row for revival on campus. In the midst of praying for revival with my friends, I felt as though the voice of God was telling me to go home and see my father. It was approximately 10:30 p.m. I asked Tom Sirotnik, my football player friend, to go with me since we were both from Long Beach. We got into my diesel VW Rabbit, which could go from 0-60 in about ten minutes, and headed down the 110 freeway. Upon entering the freeway, we noticed that the gas gauge was registering empty. This was kind of normative for a college student, so we shouldn't have been too surprised.

There were no gas stations located close to the freeway, so we prayed that God would get us to Long Beach. As we prayed, the gas gauge went from empty to full before our eyes. I looked at Tommy and said, "Are you seeing this? Look at this! Are you seeing this?" Instantly, we knew we were on an assignment for the Lord. When we arrived at my parents' house in Long Beach, my father answered the door. My dad is an amazing man; he is the peacemaker in our family. A Korean war veteran, he was at that time a stoic, non-emotional man. His first words to me were, "God sent you here, didn't He?"

"Yes, Dad," I replied. "The Lord told us to come see you tonight."

"I was going to take my life tonight at midnight," Dad informed me. "My prayer was, 'God, if you are real, then show yourself to me before midnight tonight.'" It was 11:45 p.m. when Tom and I got there, and we were able to assure my dad that Jesus was real and had heard his prayers. It was my responding to the voice of God that saved my father's life. We didn't just hear; we acted upon what we heard.

When Jesus said in John 8:32 that we would know the truth and the truth would set us free, He was talking about relational knowledge, not book knowledge. Theologian Rudolph Bultmann notes that the Greek word for "know," *ginosko*, "denotes in ordinary Greek the intelligent comprehension of an object or matter, whether this comes for the first time, or comes afresh, into the consideration of the one who grasps it ('to come to know,' 'to experience,' 'to perceive [again]') or whether it is already present ('to perceive')."[5]

Therefore, to *ginosko* something is not to know *about*, in the acquisition of head knowledge, but to know experientially in a relational context. This prophetic encounter has led me to seek God and to hear His voice for myself. It became a reality check for me that there is a God who is real, who knows me, and who loves me. My hope is that you will be encouraged to do the same with some of the tools provided in this book.

Notes

1 John Ortberg, "Seven Things I Hate About Spiritual Formation: Forget being exotic and elite; it's all about becoming more like Christ." *Christianity Today*, https://www.christianitytoday.com/pastors/2013/april-online-only/seven-things-i-hate-about-spiritual-formation.html, accessed July 24, 2018.

2 Some say Michael was the best high school football player of all time. In this video, you can see that he walks with a cane. http://www.youtube.com/watch?v=fmUN_noCV7w, accessed February 13, 2013.

3 http://www.usclegends.org/chip-banks.php, accessed February 13, 2013.

4 Prophecy is a revelatory gift that deals with a person's heart. The definition of the prophetic is taken from 1 Corinthians 14:25, which says that when one prophesies to an unbeliever "the secrets of his heart are disclosed; and so, he will fall on his face and worship God, declaring that God is certainly among you."

5 Rudolph Bultmann, *Theological Dictionary of the New Testament*, Gerhard Kittel, Geoffrey W. Bromiley and Gerhard Friedrich, eds.; electronic. (Grand Rapids, MI: Eerdmans, 1964), 689.

Chapter Two

Understanding Our Worldviews

Shallow understanding from people of good will is more frustrating than absolute misunderstanding from people of ill will.
— Martin Luther King, Jr.

We live in a time when Christianity is declining in the West. People are leaving the church in droves while the church sits back trying to get a reactive grasp of what is going on. In his book, *The Celtic Way of Evangelism*, George Hunter talks about sharing one's faith to an unbelieving culture: "When you understand the people, you will often know what to say and do, and how. When the people know that the Christians understand them, they infer that maybe the High God understands them too."[1]

Western culture today resembles in many ways the dominant culture in which the apostles and the early church and its leaders lived and ministered, a culture abounding in many different gods and worldviews. Our problem is that our modern sophistication and advances in science, communications, medicine, space travel, and technology have so distanced us cognitively from the people and the world of the first century that we have lost all sense of connection with them. How could we in the 21st century possibly have anything in common with a first-century Roman, Greek, or Jew? Our ethno-centrism (thinking we are the best) and religiocentrism (thinking our beliefs are the best) deceive us into believing that everything about us—our culture, our norms, our values, and the way we do things—are the finest and best that humanity has ever produced. But we need to ask ourselves, Has the human heart changed that much since the first century?

The disciples walked into a world teeming with a plethora of gods. Acts 17 finds the apostle Paul in Athens taking note of the many statues representing the multiplicity of gods worshiped by the people in the city. One monument in particular, erected by Epimenides to recognize the "unknown God," Paul uses later, when addressing a gathering of Greeks on Mars Hill, as a focal point in preaching Jesus to them as the "unknown God" they have been seeking.

The Greeks had a large pantheon of gods and a vibrant culture that maintained its dominance despite Rome's conquest of Greece. Many of these ancient statues of the gods still exist and can be seen in Italy and Greece and other places in Europe that once were part of the ancient Roman Empire. The Romans largely adopted the Greek gods for themselves but gave them new names, except for Apollo, whose name the Romans retained (these are only a few):

- Zeus: The sky-god and king of the gods; Roman name: Jupiter or Jove
- Hera: Powerful goddess often jealous, vicious, and spiteful. Roman name: Juno
- Aphrodite: Goddess of love, beauty and desire. Roman name: Venus
- Apollo: God of light, healing, music, poetry, plague, prophecy, and more.
- Ares: God of war and bloodshed. Roman name: Mars
- Artemis: Goddess of hunting, wilderness, animals and childbirth. Roman name: Diana
- Athena: Goddess of wisdom and skill, warfare and tactics. Roman name: Minerva
- Demeter: Goddess of farming, the harvest, and fertility. Roman name: Ceres

- Dionysus: God of wine, parties, festivals; madness and ecstasy. Roman name: Bacchus
- Hades: King of the underworld and god of the dead. Roman name: Pluto

Don't you think, when we consider the characteristics of these "deities," that we can identify many of those same traits as prevalent in our Western culture today? Narcissism, the obsession with beauty and good looks? Nature and its protection at all costs? The attainment of scientific knowledge? Hedonism and the pursuit of pleasure? While we may not call these traits gods today, they are still powerful forces that drive many people to seek pleasure, happiness, success, and wealth through their use.

Our Western society today is comprised largely of a theologically-blended group of people, many of whom are skeptics who follow a postmodern, metamodern, or even pagan worldview. A worldview is our reality of how we see the world. It is "a basic set of beliefs that guide action."[2] Everyone has a worldview that determines the way they look at life. Worldviews are like eyeglasses of different tints—dark-shaded, lightly-shaded, rose-shaded, polarized, etc.—that color the way we see the world; they validate in our minds what we believe the world is like. Research, news, and political commentaries are often influenced by the worldview that a person holds, and this sometimes can spark an epidemic of false news. Some people hold a deterministic view of the world, that the current state of the world is due to "antecedent conditions," while others are more pragmatic in their outlook, adopting a worldview that, as Creswell comments, "arises out of actions, situations, and consequences... There is a concern with applications—what works—and solutions to problems."[3] We (and our culture) think and act according to our worldview because we believe it to be reality. Whether or not we are cognitive of it, our worldview, regardless of what it is, skews our objectivity in how we think of the world.

If you are a baby boomer, there is a strong chance that you have a modernist mindset or worldview, which means that you believe in facts as reality, absolute truth, objective teaching, and values that are based in biblical truths. Postmodernism, however, denies the existence of absolute truth and frowns on traditional authority and power; nihilism is a major part of this skeptical mindset. Metamodernists base reality on their feelings and are heavily influenced by what their peer group thinks. As a result, social media is a primary determinant of their relational reality. Pagans (yes, they are still with us today), hold beliefs that are rooted in the supernatural, but not the God of the Bible. What is the best method for Christians to use in reaching the unsaved in such a polyglot culture?

How can we best communicate the gospel message today in a postmodern worldview where truth is relative, meaning that there are no absolutes; "truth" is whatever you decide it is for you? Or in a metamodern worldview, which says that our emotional reactions to things determine our reality. Metamodernism has been defined as a "'structure of feeling' that oscillates between modernism and postmodernism."[4] According to an online Huffington Post article, "Metamodernism is particularly useful at helping us understand the internet because it's the cultural philosophy of the digital age."[5] Its characteristic as a response to postmodernism was foreshadowed in the 1981 experimental film *My Dinner with Andre*. In the film, "Andre Gregory describes—for nearly two hours—metamodern performance art...and a 'reconstructive' metamodern mindset exponentially more present and actionable in the 2010s than it was in the 1980s." Movie critic Roger Ebert, in a four-star review, "summarized Gregory's philosophy as a belief that 'the quest for transcendence is important even if there is, in fact, no transcendence to be found'—an incomplete but not unreasonable summary of how metamodernism manifests today, if we take 'transcendence' to mean 'transcending the conditions that postmodern culture artificially imposes upon us.'"[6]

Thus, postmodernism is a reaction to modernism; truth becomes relative. With metamodernism, feelings become reality. Postmodernism, with its relativism and cynicism, laid the groundwork for metamodernism. Metamodernism is not a new term; it was coined in the 70's. Yet, today it has become the new worldview for our youth. It is a kind of informed nativism brought on by social media and the internet. A metamodernist searching for truth will go to the internet or social media to foster community. Metamodernist people find their community online. Digital connection is their reality, and isolation from real people becomes normative. Metamodernism is a structure of feelings that oscillate between truth and feelings. Mark Sayer, in his book The New Powers, summarizes the basic values or worldview of metamodernism:

1) The highest good is individual freedom, happiness, self-definition, and self-expression.
2) Traditions, religions, received wisdom, regulations, and social ties that restrict individual freedom, happiness, self-definition, and self-expression must be reshaped, deconstructed, or destroyed.
3) The world will inevitably improve as the scope of individual freedom grows. Technology-in particular the Internet – will motor this progression toward utopia.
4) The primary social ethic is tolerance of everyone's self-defined quest for individual freedom and self-expression. Any deviation from this ethic of tolerance is dangerous and must not be tolerated. Therefore, social justice is less about economic class inequality, and more about issues of equality relating to individual identity, self-expression, and personal autonomy.
5) Humans are inherently good.
6) Large-scale structures and institutions are suspicious at best and evil at worst.
7) Forms of external authority are rejected and personal authenticity is lauded.[7]

The apologetic for the modernist mindset is that of a rational or logical belief system; truth can be discovered and then applied. For postmoderns, however, truth is relative; "truth" is whatever each person individually believes is true. So postmoderns usually can't be won to Christ by utilizing objective truth arguments. As Stanley Hauerwas explains, "The invitation to join such a life [in Christ] is made not on the assumption that there is something wrong with the others' beliefs, but it is made because we are all sinners and through participation in this community we have the possibility of finding redemption."[8] In other words, to say that something is wrong with what another person thinks is anti-postmodern thought because to them truth is whatever they believe it to be. They must be reached another way.

Utilizing a traditional modernist apologetic is of increasingly limited value in bringing a person to Christ today because in today's culture many people regard truth as relative, fluid, changeable from one person to the next or from one day to the next. Because of this massive cultural shift, traditional methods of evangelism with their focus on absolute truth claims are not as effective today as they once were. For example, not long ago a young adult in my church traveled overseas on an evangelistic trip with a well-known campus group. They used a traditional form of evangelism, a type of survey questionnaire that they administered to over 5000 college students in Australia. The intent of this survey was to lead students to Christ. Although this was a time-proven method that had seen great success in the United States but, Australia was a different culture. Out of 5000 surveys, not a single conversion was recorded. Alcoholics Anonymous defines insanity as doing the same thing over and over again and expecting a different result. If one approach has stopped working despite repeated attempts, it should be replaced even if it has worked successfully in the past. In light of the substantial worldview shift in our culture, our methodology of evangelism must shift also; not the gospel message, but the manner of presenting the gospel message.

If you are a modernist in your worldview, you will become frustrated trying to relate to a metamodernist because giving them facts is not on their radar. They can go to the internet and find rebuttals to your argument. This is the paradigm shift of culture that we are facing today. Actually, this is a perfect set up by Jesus to bring His Spirit to a lost, hopeless, and hurting world.

In contrast to the fruitless Australia mission, a group of Youth With A Mission (YWAM) students went to Germany to evangelize immigrant Muslims. In four weeks they led over five hundred people to the Lord. What was the difference? The group in Germany experienced divine encounters while praying for the sick and operating in the prophetic that drew many Muslims to Christ. Muslims have always believed that Jesus was a prophet, but these Muslims in Germany had an encounter with the Son of God who intervened in their world. He became more than a prophet to them. Good prophets don't lie, and Jesus claimed to be the Christ.

These two examples illustrate a modernist evangelistic model versus Jesus' charismata model. Jesus said in Mark 16:17 that signs and wonders would follow the preaching of the gospel. Why do we need these things in our life? For one thing, signs, wonders, and miracles attest to Jesus (Acts 2:22). The Western church today has many programs that attest to Christ as Savior and Lord and yet are dwindling in effectiveness. Why would this be? The main reasons are their lack of accompanying spiritual power and the fact that the message as so often presented seems completely irrelevant to non-Christians.

Programs without the Spirit will become dead, dry ritual. A ritual is "any practice or pattern of behavior regularly performed in a set manner."⁹ the danger here is that established ritual can easily take precedence over the organic flow of the Holy Spirit. Why don't dead works cut it? Simply put, our God is a living God; He is not into dead things. He makes all things new. Not that the old is bad necessarily, but we need to be creative. Solomon tells us that it takes wisdom to win souls (Prov. 11:30). For example, William Booth, the founder of the Salvation Army, adopted the practice of marching into towns with a band playing instruments. In his time, this was an innovative and highly effective approach to reaching the lost. Many people were won to Christ through Booth's creative modes of evangelism. Aimee Semple McPherson, the founder of the Foursquare Gospel church, once rode a motorcycle onto the stage for an illustrated sermon. Times have changed. Today, a "salvation band" marching down the street probably would not be the best approach to winning souls, and riding a motorcycle in church likely would be dismissed as a "stunt."

When we bring in the gifts of the Spirit (as delineated in 1 Corinthians12), we bring in the supernatural power of God that cuts through all the philosophical barriers that people erect and leads them to the reality of the cross of Christ.[10] It is not we who wield this power, but Christ in us; by its very nature, this is a God-breathed intervention.

Aristotle's rhetorical model of communication consists of three necessary components for effective communication: the communicator, the message, and the audience.[11] We have a wonderful message that our audience needs to hear but cannot because our method of communication raises suspicion in their minds. The world is "on to" our programs and assume that we have an ulterior motive. "What do they want from me?" "Are they trying to manipulate me?" These are the kinds of vibes that many relativistic-minded non-Christ followers pick up on.

Jesus is the master communicator. We see this throughout the Gospels, but especially with the woman at the well (Jn. 4). Here was a woman who had been rejected by her community because of her sinful lifestyle. She was relationally broken, reduced to fetching water during the hottest part of the day so that she would not have to interact with anyone else. She was shamed in her brokenness. Jesus, knowing everything that was going on in her life, overcame all of her objections one by one. He prophesied to her about her lifestyle and marital history, which amazed her. Analyzing this according to Aristotle's model, the woman (audience) heard the prophetic words (message) of Jesus (communicator), which led her to the revelation that Jesus is the Christ. After such an encounter as this, a more traditional apologetic can be applied that gives reasons why Jesus is who He says He is. In other words, in a postmodern-metamodern culture, the prophetic becomes the apologetic because it proves to people that Jesus is who He says He is.

What if we used experiential encounters the way Jesus did, using the prophetic and healing to stir up faith in the skeptical or insecure mind? When I say "experiential encounter," I am referring to an encounter with the living God, not an emotional experience or event. Bill Johnson's church, Bethel, in Redding, California, uses a form of prophetic evangelism called Treasure Hunting. Treasure Hunting encourages one to hear God speak and then act upon it. What I like about this is that they go out into their community to bring the reality of Christ to the lost. It's not an event in the church but on the streets. Jesus modeled this approach in His encounter with Zacchaeus. Jesus went to the broken, the shamed, and the rejected to prophesy to them about who He is.

Once I was speaking at a YWAM Disciple Training School in Portland, Oregon. I lectured several hours a day and at night took the students out to practice what they were taught. There was a young Russian student named Sasha in the class. Sasha always wore a defiant expression that radiated, "I do not want to be here." One night when we went out, Sasha told me that he didn't believe a thing I had taught in class that day. I responded by telling him that we should see at least two miracles that night. If that statement sounds presumptuous, it really isn't. I live in Montana, a state with more cows than people, so my faith was pretty high that we would encounter many hurting people in downtown Portland.

We took two steps, literally, and bumped into two girls. I told them that we were praying for people and asked if we could pray for them.

"We don't speak English," they said.

"What do you speak?" I asked.

"Russian."

"That's awesome," I replied, "because Sasha is Russian."

I then heard the still small voice of the Lord (1 Ki. 19:11) instruct us to ask the girl if she was in a car wreck recently. "Were you in a car wreck recently," Sasha asked in Russian.

"Da" (yes), she replied, "a week ago."

With Sasha again translating for me, I asked, "Is your neck messed up as a result of the accident?"

"Da."

Right there on the street, we prayed for her. Immediately, her pain went away, and we led her to the Lord.

We walked about a quarter of a block down the street and ran into three homeless people, two men and one girl. I suddenly had a tremendous empathetic emotion come upon me for the girl. Now, I have been married 31 years, have five daughters, and a grandson, so this was a father-for-a-hurting-daughter kind of feeling. I approached the girl and introduced myself and Sasha to her and her friends. I felt like I heard the Lord say that her ex-boyfriend had abused her and that she had been out on the streets for several weeks and had not slept in days. When I mentioned these things to her, she confirmed that they were true then asked, "How do you know this?" I told her that it was normal for followers of Jesus to hear His voice (Jn. 10:27) and asked if I could pray for her. As I started to pray for her, peace came upon her in a dramatic way. I could see the presence of God's embrace upon her. She was amazed and in shock, but also peacefully set free from fear. She had started crying, but then looked up at me.

"You have this strange mystical presence all over you," she said. "What is that?"

Jokingly, I told her it was dandruff, but then seriously I said, "It's the Holy Spirit. He likes to hang around followers of Jesus. Would you like the same thing in your life?"

That night, within one hour, we had seen two people healed of both physical and emotional damage (Ps. 147:3) and three people come to Jesus. Today, Sasha still calls me regularly for advice and prayer. God not only touched those girls on the street of Portland, but Sasha as well. Sasha went from head knowledge to heart knowledge that day. His faith went from the God of the stories to the God who intervenes in one's own life.

In a postmodern, metamodern culture such as in the West, the charismata apologetic is the gifts of the Holy Spirit (1 Cor.12:8-10) that reveal to people the reality of Jesus. The gifts of the Spirit, particularly the prophetic gift, miracles, and healing, allow nonbelievers to acknowledge that God is real. This was the intent of the gifts, to make God real, to attest to His reality. Acts 2:22 tells us that God "attested" His Son "with miracles and wonders and signs."

Paul reveals the purpose of the prophetic in 1 Corinthians 14:25. When we prophesy, Paul says, "the secrets of his (the unbeliever or ungifted) heart are disclosed; and so he will fall on his face and worship God, declaring that God is certainly among you." Did you catch that? Whenever we prophesy, unbelievers will say "God is really among you." In other words, God is real and He is with us and in us. If this is the modus operandi for Paul and Luke when encountering a culture with many gods, then maybe this will work today for us. Watchman Nee wrote in *The Release of the Spirit*, "Do we impress people with ourselves, or with the Lord? Do we draw people to our teaching, or to the Lord? This is genuinely vital. It determines the value of all our work and labor." The gifts impress people with the Lord. If you try using them so that people will be impressed by you, then you are in for a fall.

Notes

1   George G. Hunter III, *The Celtic Way of Evangelism: How Christianity Can Reach the West...Again.* (Nashville: Abingdon Press, 2000), 20.

2   E.G. Guba, *The Paradigm Dialog.* (Newbury Park: Sage, 1990), 17.

3   John W. Creswell and J. David Creswell, *Research Design: Qualitative, Quantitative, and Mixed Methods Approaches, Fifth Edition.* (Los Angeles: SAGE Publications, Inc., 2018), 10.

4   "Metamodernism," https://en.wikipedia.org/wiki/Metamodernism, accessed January 3, 2019.

5   Seth Abramson, "What is Metamodernism?" https://www.huffingtonpost. com/entry/what-is-metamodernism_us_586e7075e4b0a5e600a788cd,   accessed January 3, 2019.

6   Seth Abramson, "What is Metamodernism?"

7   Mark Sayer, *Disappearing Church: From Cultural Relevance to Gospel Resilience.* (Chicago: Moody Publishers, 2016), 16-17.

8   Stanley Hauerwas, *A Community of Character: Toward a Constructive Christian Social Ethic.* (Notre Dame: University of Notre Dame Press, 1981),105.

9   *Random House Kernerman Webster's College Dictionary.* S.v. "ritual." https:// www.thefreedictionary.com/ritual, accessed December 17, 2018.

10 Glen Berteau, *Christianity Lite: Stop Drinking a Watered-Down Gospel.* (Lake Mary: Passio, 2013), 62. Many modern people don't pray because they trust advances in technology and medicine to solve their problems.

11 Aristotle, *The Rhetoric of Aristotle,* trans., Lane Cooper. (Englewood Cliffs: Prentice-Hall, 1960), 37.

Chapter Three

The Role of the Holy Spirit Today

What is the role of the Holy Spirit in modern Christianity today, and how does the Holy Spirit relate to the message that Jesus came to communicate? In America and Western Europe, Christianity is on the decline, but is gaining influence in the "two-thirds world": Asia, Africa, and South America.[1] As the western church tries to get a grasp on its state of influence in culture, the churches of the two-thirds world are thriving. Unlike the western church, their paradigm of ministry is founded on the charismata, i.e., healings, exorcisms, prophecy, and miracles.[2]

George Barna has stated that in America this year less than two percent of congregations will hear a message on the Holy Spirit.[3] Asian and African theologians have complained that the American approach to church is irrelevant to Asian and African cultures.[4]

It is my belief that the apologetic has shifted, and we must embrace the old to relate to the new. We must do the things that Jesus did to touch the heart of people today. In metamodernism we need to go to the heart and then to the head. The Holy Spirit has not changed. The question is whether we have changed in how we view the Holy Spirit. As I mentioned, Jesus demonstrated for us how to touch the hurt and broken. He did this in John 4 with the woman at the well. Jesus sat with a woman of questionable repute, a cultural *faux pas*. He then prophesied to her about her marital condition, leading her to the revelation that He was Messiah. She had an encounter that led her to the reality of Jesus. People want and need an encounter with the all-powerful God, not an encounter with an authoritative system. Encounters with Jesus bring revelation as to who He is; then it is time to present sound biblical reasons for our faith. An encounter with Jesus should lead people to a surrendered life to Jesus in the revelation that He is the Christ. Experience should not be the main focal point of the encounter, but the launching pad into His kingdom.

As D. A. Carson notes:

> Modernism is often pictured as pursuing truth, absolutism, linear thinking, rationalism, certainty, the cerebral as opposed to the effective--which in turn breeds arrogance, and inflexibility, the lust to be right, the desire to control. Postmodernism, by contrast, recognizes how much of what we "know" is shaped by the culture in which we live, is controlled by emotions and aesthetics and heritage, and in fact can only be intelligently held as part of a common tradition, without overbearing claims to be true or right.[5]

In his book, *The Listening Society*, Hanzi Freinacht observes:

> People are hurt and afraid at a subtle psychological level—and are therefore self-absorbed, incapable of taking on larger perspectives and incapable of acting upon the very real long-term risks that are threatening our global civilization. We must, at all cost, make the world population much, much happier in the deepest sense of the word...
>
> Let's return to the main argument. People are hurting as hell. It matters. We should do something to make them happier, if we can."[6]

Use of the prophetic involves invading culture, emotions, heritage, and traditions without trying to be true or right. This approach appeals to metamodernists because it goes to their feelings, and thus to their concept of reality in the world, but without trying to exercise authoritative power over them, which they would view as intolerant. The prophetic reveals the secrets of a person's heart. As we have already seen, 1 Corinthians 14:25 says that when one prophesies to an unbeliever or an ungifted man, "the secrets of his heart are disclosed; and so he will fall on his face and worship God, declaring that God is certainly among you." The prophetic allows people to experience God and touches the core of who they are. This is as relevant today as it was in Jesus' day, a real encounter with a real God that leads people to Christ.

To touch people today, we need a new generation of people who hear God's voice and know Him personally to bring the reality of Christ. Jon Ruthven says this about the message of Jesus and the religious leaders of Jesus' time:

The conflict between the message of Jesus and the doctrine of the religious leaders of his time (and our time) focused on the central issue of how (or if) one hears from God…Put another way, the difference between the message of the Bible and the message of traditional (human) religion is the emphasis on two different kinds of knowing: the biblical "knowing," that is, the experience of God, vs. merely knowing information about him.[7]

The gifts should bring people to Christ, yet some have said that God quit doing this long ago. That point of view essentially changes the nature of God from the great "I Am" to the great "I Was." The Bible presents a picture of a God who is all-powerful; the Alpha and the Omega who is the same yesterday, today, and forever. Yet there are some who insist that His power is limited in today's culture. They act as though they believe that God gave us the Bible and then vanished from our lives, leaving us to fend for ourselves until He comes back. That is a kind of Bible deism.

Under classic deism, God created the world complete and then moved away from it to leave humanity on its own. Dallas Willard, who coined the phrase "Bible deism," states that a Bible deist believes that "God gave us the Bible and then went away, leaving us to make what we could of it, with no individual communication either through the Bible or otherwise."[8] Bible deism is much like the doctrine of the Sadducees, who limited their belief in the supernatural. Josephus confirms that the Sadducees denied the resurrection, the immortality of the soul, eternal rewards, or the "world to come."[9] The Sadducees kept their focus on the status quo of the nation of Israel in this world and not the next. Cessationism, a theology that believes all the gifts ended with the death of the last apostle, changes the promise of God that He would be with us always and tell us things to come (Jn. 16:13). Peter, however, proclaimed that the outpouring of the Holy Spirit would continue until the Lord quit calling people to Himself. In the context of the day of Pentecost and people getting saved, speaking in tongues, and acting like they were drunk, Peter said: "For the promise is for you and for your children and for all who are far off, everyone whom the Lord our God calls to himself" (Acts 2:39 ESV). Peter makes it absolutely clear that what was happening on the day of Pentecost would continue to happen until the last person on earth to be saved entered the kingdom of heaven.

Notes

1   Vivian S. Park, "Scholars Find Decline of Christianity in the West one of the transforming moments in the history of religion worldwide," in *The Christian Post*. http://www.christianpost.com/news/scholars-find-decline-of-christianity-in-the-west-19971/ (March 6th, 2004). In 1900, Africa had 10 million Christians, today it has 360 million followers of Christ. According to researcher David Barrett, author of *World Christian Encyclopedia*, Africa is gaining 8.4 million new Christians a year.

2   Craig S. Keener, *Miracles: The Credibility of the New Testament Accounts* (Grand Rapids: Baker Academic, 2011), 296-297. Keener says that as many as 90% of conversions in China are the result of healings and miracles.

3   George Barna, "The Last Unregulated Wild Frontier of Influence," http://www.georgebarna.com/2010/03/the-last-unregulated-wild-frontier-of-influence/ (March 10th, 2010), accessed October 3, 2013. Barna also makes the claim that in the United States in the next twenty years, 70% of believers will leave the local church and become involved with home churches or some other venue of worship.

4   Keener, *Miracles*, 215.

5   D. A Carson, *Becoming Conversant with the Emerging Church.* (Grand Rapids: Zondervan, 2005), 27.

6   Hanzi Freinacht, *The Listening Society: A Metamodern Guide to Politics, Book One (Metamodern Guides) (Volume 1)* (Metamoderna aps, www.metamoderna. org, 2017)

7   Jon Mark Ruthven, *What's Wrong with Protestant Theology? Tradition vs. Biblical Emphasis.* (Tulsa: Word & Spirit Press, 2013).

8   Dallas Willard, *Hearing God: Developing a Conversational Relationship with God, Updated and Expanded by Jan Johnson.* (Downers Grove: InterVarsity Press, 1984, 1993, 1999, 2012), 142.

9   Josephus, *Antiquities*, 18.1.4 [16]; *Wars*, 2.8.14 [165].

Chapter Four

Miracles: The Validation of the Gospel Message

It is impossible on reasonable grounds to disbelieve miracles.
— Blaise Pascal

Miracles have always been the validation of the gospel established by Jesus and carried on by His disciples, as recorded in the four Gospels and the Book of Acts, and reported in the epistles of the New Testament. The author of Hebrews authenticated this method of evangelism by relying upon his observation of how Jesus did things: "[H]ow will we escape if we neglect so great a salvation? After it was at the first spoken through the Lord, it was confirmed to us by those who heard, ***God also testifying with them, both by signs and wonders and by various miracles and by gifts of the Holy Spirit*** according to His own will" (Heb. 2:3–4, emphasis added). Unfortunately, some cessationist theologians (people who believe that the gifts have ended), claim that miracles prove nothing.[1] In actuality, miracles are what the Father used to prove His son's deity (Acts 2:22), and today He graces us still with the ability to do this ourselves to show the world that He is real.

The apostle Paul makes it clear that God's method for validating the authenticity of the preached message of the gospel of Christ was the powerful demonstration of signs, wonders, miracles, and gifts of the Holy Spirit, i.e., the charismata:

For I will not presume to speak of anything except what Christ has accomplished through me, ***resulting in the obedience of the Gentiles by word and deed, in the power of signs and wonders, in the power of the Spirit***; so that from Jerusalem and round about as far as Illyricum I have fully preached the gospel of Christ (Rom. 15:18–19, emphasis added).

Miracles bring glory to God and validate a person's ministry. In Matthew 9:8, after a paralytic man is healed, Matthew observes, "But when the crowds saw *this,* they were awestruck, and glorified God, who had given such authority to men." Thus, this miracle brought glory both to God and to the one working the miracle. Miracles are God's way of establishing and confirming His calling upon a person while at the same time causing them to acknowledge God. As R. C. Sproul comments, "A miracle, technically and correctly defined, is a work that only God can do, such as bringing something out of nothing or bringing life out of death...So rather than proving the existence of God, the biblical miracles serves to authenticate the messenger sent from God."[2] When people witness a miracle, they begin to glorify God, and it brings credibility to the message of the messenger. God is clearly using miracles in the two-thirds world today to bring people to Himself.

In Africa, nearly all Christians, including theologians, reject Western Anti-supernaturalism.[3] In Ethiopia, 83 percent of Christians came to Christ as a result of experiencing a healing or an exorcism.[4] "In the twentieth century, Christianity in Africa exploded from an estimated population of eight or nine million in 1900 (8 to 9%) to some 335 million in 2000 (45%), marking a shift in the 'center of gravity of Christianity' from the West to Latin America, parts of Asia and Africa."[5] In China, some surveys record that 90 percent of new believers cite healing as a reason for their conversion.[6] The paradigm that is changing the 10/40 window is one that embraces the charismata, or the power of God at work in our lives today.[7]

In contrast, the American church has embraced a "seeker model" of doing church, leaving some feeling dissatisfied with church.[8] Essential areas of spiritual disciplines such as Bible reading, sharing one's faith, and a paradigm acknowledging anything of the Holy Spirit are missing. Dr. David Yonggi Cho, who established Yoido Full Gospel Church in South Korea, a megachurch with 750,000 members, feels the lack of emphasis given to the miraculous is a cover up to justify the powerlessness of the church. "This lack of attention to God's power is grievous to the Spirit. Signs, wonders, and the power of the Holy Spirit are essential for successful preaching of the gospel."[9]

In the 1980s, membership in the American church dropped almost 10 percent; the 1990s were even worse, with a drop of 12 percent. "Some denominations are reporting a 40 percent drop in their membership. And now, over half way through the first decade of the 21st century, we are seeing the figures drop even more!" says Dr. Richard J. Krejcir of the Schaeffer Institute.[10] The Assemblies of God U.S. Missions states, "Every year more than 4,000 churches close their doors compared to just over 1,000 new church starts!"[11] The United States Census Bureau Records confirms the denominational reports with these startling statistics:

- There were about 4,500 new churches started between 1990 and 2000, with a twenty-year average of nearly 1,000 a year.
- Every year, 2,750,000 church members fall into inactivity. This translates into the realization that people are leaving the church. Our research has found that they are leaving as hurting and wounded victims—of some kind of abuse, disillusionment, or just plain neglect!
- From 1990 to 2000, the combined membership of all Protestant denominations in the US declined by almost 5,000,000 members (9.5%), while the population increased by 24,000,000 (11%).
- In 1900 there was a ratio of 27 churches per 10,000 people; in 2000 there were 11 churches per 10,000 people in America!"

- Given the declining numbers and closures of churches as compared to new church starts, there should have been over 38,000 new churches commissioned to keep up with the *population* growth.
- The United States now ranks third following China and India, in the number of people who are not professing Christians; in other words, the U.S. is becoming an ever-increasing unreached people group.
- Half of all churches in the U.S. did not add any new members to their ranks in the last two years.[12]

Wow, the church in the USA needs a major revival doesn't it? If my stock portfolio was going down 10-12% a year, I would want to try a different investment strategy. Things don't seem to be working too well for us in the area of church planting or growth in the Western hemisphere. This is not a book about church growth, but one on effective ways to approach and apply the gospel message in the postmodern/metamodern culture that is challenging the Western church.

In his book, *How to Win Secular People*, George G. Hunter compares the first three centuries of Christianity to our current religious environment in the West. He says that in the Christian movement's first three centuries, communicating the gospel effectively required the overcoming of four obstacles:

1. Facing a population with no knowledge of the gospel, the Christian movement had to inform people of the story of Jesus, the good news, its claims, and its offer.
2. Facing hostile populations and the persecution of the state, the church had to win friends and influence people to a positive attitude toward the movement.
3. Facing an Empire with several entrenched religions, the Christians had to convince people of Christianity's truth, or at least its plausibility.
4. Since entry into the faith is by an act of will, Christians had to invite people to adopt faith and join the messianic community and follow Jesus as Lord.[13]

Donald Soper says, "Not one in every ten people has the remotest idea of what you and I within the church mean by religion," and this is exactly what the early church had to face.[14]

If Hunter is correct, we have an opportunity to present the gospel to a group of people who do not know the gospel story, just like the early church. We are in a culture that invites a different apologetic. People are becoming unaware of the stories of the Bible. Alan Walker says:

> So today there is almost a complete ignorance of what the Christian gospel really is. You see, Christian knowledge and awareness are now the echo of an echo of an echo--too faint to be heard. This means, for example, a feeling of awkwardness, even embarrassment, at entering a sacred building. There is ignorance in the ways of Christian worship. Therefore, such people no longer desire to enter churches. It means an almost complete ignorance of Christian stories, biblical references, and the traditional language of the pulpit."[15]

In many ways, things today are parallel to Paul's early church experience. Few in Paul's day knew the story of Christ. Paul was presenting the gospel to people groups who had never heard of Jesus; his mode of evangelism was presenting the gospel in power and by a demonstration of the Holy Spirit. Writing to the Thessalonians, Paul said, "For when we brought you the Good News, it was not only with words but also with power, for the Holy Spirit gave you full assurance that what we said was true. And you know of our concern for you from the way we lived when we were with you" (1 Th. 1:5 NLT).

Paul's presentation of the gospel did not come in word only. There is no hint here that Paul was discounting the spoken word. His assertion, rather, was that the gospel was communicated more than just verbally. Demonstrations of power, the work of the Holy Spirit, and the full conviction of the messengers worked with the words to provide the validation of his belief in Christ. Paul gave the Thessalonians a cogent and convincing presentation of the gospel with both power and word. The gospel presented in Thessalonica came with power, with the Holy Spirit, and with deep conviction to convince an uninformed group of people of the reality of Christ, and the word. People saw it, experienced it, and were converted to it because they experienced it. They saw the reality of it, not just the theory of it.

But how were these experiences more convincing than words alone? There is a saying that we use a lot at our church: "Information without application never leads to transformation." Paul applied what He saw Christ and the apostles do, which led to transforming the culture. Several passages in Paul's letters (Rom. 15:17–19; 2 Cor. 12:12) and in Acts (14:3; 16:17–18; 19:6, 11–12) record the miraculous events that accompanied the Pauline gospel. The word used for "power" (*dunamis*) is also one of the words used in the Gospels for Jesus' miracles. It was God's power, not Paul's, that was demonstrated among the Thessalonians in 1 Thessalonians1: 5.[16] The *dunamis* of God is for us to be a witness of His kingdom (Acts 1:8).

If the message of the gospel that Paul preached was in demonstrating God's power and the Holy Spirit, what message is the United States church conveying today to the lost? "Hey, Christianity is so cool! Just look at our awesome service production, our amazing worship, lights, and dramas. And how about our great social media footprint." This may be the ethos of many of our churches today.

Walter Grundmann says this about the power of Jesus: "The history of Jesus is the history of Christ because the kingdom of God comes with Him."[17] *Dunamis* is the word used for power and can be translated as potential for functioning in some way, power, might, strength, force, capability; specifically, it is the power that works wonders.[18] *Dunamis* is an empowerment by God to His people to perform miracles to an unbelieving culture and thus become an empowered witness or an ambassador of Christ's unseen kingdom, to bring the reality to the lost.

Paul's approach to evangelizing unreached people groups was not just in the rhetoric of words, good programs, social justice, and really cool stage and worship presentations for the fostering of hip community, but also in proving the gospel by signs, wonders, and miracles. Thank you, Jesus, that we have so many amazing ways to present the presentation of the gospel in whatever culture we are in. What if we had all that, but also became Spirit sensitive?

In a Spirit-sensitive church, it's not about the program that everyone else is doing. It's about hearing from God for you and doing what He tells you to do at the place where you are. God is a creative God and He has a creative idea for you and your church. Moving in the gifts can make us uncomfortable. It takes risks; it takes getting out of the boat and into the raging sea of culture. It might feel awkward at first, but we need to be naturally supernatural, not weird. I like what John Wimber used to say: "Faith is spelled R-I-S-K." Faith impresses God; it gets His attention. When we get in a rut, we only look at the walls around us; we become myopic in how we see things. When we take risks for God, we position ourselves for the divine hand of God to act.

Paul's message was backed up by demonstrative acts of the Holy Spirit. Most Christians today do not have a supernatural worldview of God and His kingdom. George Barna said:

> Four out of ten (American) Christians (40%) strongly agreed that Satan "is not a living being but is a symbol of evil." An additional two out of ten Christians (19%) said they "agree somewhat" with that perspective. A minority of Christians indicated that they believe Satan is real by disagreeing with the statement: one-quarter (26%) disagreed strongly and about one-tenth (9%) disagreed somewhat. The remaining (8%) were not sure what they believe about the existence of Satan.[19]

In the same study, regarding the Holy Spirit, Barna found that:

> Much like their perceptions of Satan, most Christians do not believe that the Holy Spirit is a living force, either. Overall, (38%) strongly agreed and (20%) agreed somewhat that the Holy Spirit is "a symbol of God's power or presence but is not a living entity." Just one-third of

Christians disagreed that the Holy Spirit is not a living force (9% disagreed somewhat, 25% disagreed strongly) while (9%) were not sure.[20]

We have a culture in the American church that has an unbiblical view of the Holy Spirit and demonic influences. This may be the result of our theology, our teaching, or simply uncertainty, since we might not personally have experienced these things.

The Bible speaks clearly about the unseen domain of angels, demons, spirits, and miracles. For much of the United States church, the supernatural is symbolic and theoretical rather than practical reality. We have psychology that explains away oppression. We have medicine to heal the sick. Our dependence resides more with us than with God. Most American Christians do not believe in the supernatural because they have not seen it demonstrated in their churches and feel no need for it.

While today there is a growing and thriving church in the two-thirds world that has a paradigm for 1 Thessalonians 1:5, that paradigm generally has failed to penetrate American church culture. Is it possible that we have walked away from a biblically empowered model of reaching people for Christ? A model demonstrated by Jesus and his disciples that bring us the kingdom of God by *dunamis* power? Have we embraced a Sophist model of ministry today?[21]

In Paul's day Sophists were people who were well-trained in speech and utilized teaching and rhetoric to convey their thoughts to their audience. One of the reasons the gospel spread so quickly in the first century is that the early church did more than just talk or philosophize about issues. They weren't involved with politics, but with the everyday people. Paul did not rely upon rhetoric, but on God's power as the authenticating apologetic for the gospel of Christ.

Raymond Brown comments about the Book of Mark:

First, the miracle stories are an integral part of the Gospel narrative: Almost half of the Marcan account of the public ministry (200 of 425 verses of Mk 1-10) is concerned with the miraculous."[22]

He goes on to say:

The Evangelists show no more amazement at nature miracles than at healings, nor any more difficulty in accepting them. In a worldview where not only sickness and death but also natural catastrophe represents the power of Satan, the intervention of the Kingdom of God would require a demonstration of power in the realm of nature as well as in that of human existence."[23]

Notes

1 James Montgomery Boice, "A Better Way: The Power of the Word and Spirit," in Michael S. Horton, ed., *Power Religion: The Selling Out of the Evangelical Church?* (Chicago: Moody Press, 1992), 127-128.

2 R. C. Sproul, *John, St. Andrew's Expositional Commentary.* (Lake Mary: Reformation Trust Publishing, 2009), 107.

3 Keener, *Miracles,* 217.

4 Donald A. McGavran, "Divine Healing and Church Growth," in *Signs and Wonders Today: The Story of Fuller Theological Seminary's Remarkable Course on Spiritual Power,* C. Peter Wagner, ed., (Altamonte Springs: Creation House, 1987),75.

5 http://www.christianity.com/ChurchHistory/11630859/, accessed January 4, 2019.

6 Edmond Tang, "Yellers' and Healers: Pentecostalism and the Study of Grassroots Christianity in China" (Regnum Studies in Missions AJPSS 3, Oxford: Regnum; Baguio City Philippines: APTS Press, 2005),467-86.

7 George Otis, Jr. *The Last of the Giants.* (Grand Rapids: Chosen, 1991) 244.

8 "Watch Bill Hybels," REVEAL, 15 Nov 2007, http://revealnow.com/story.asp?storyid=49, accessed 6/012/13. Greg Hawkings, *REVEAL: Where Are You?"* (Chicago: Willow Creek Association, 2009),13. Greg is a staff pastor at Willow Creek. Bill Hybels acknowledges that Willow Creek did not appreciate the dissatisfaction expressed by some of the strongest Christ-followers in his congregation. The kingdom impact of training and encouraging all Christ-followers to devote themselves to a daily discipline of personal spiritual practices was not fully implemented into the Seeker model. Currently, they are working on methods that will better help disciple new believers.

9 Paul Yonggi Cho, with R. Whitney Manzano, *The Fourth Dimension, Vol. Two: More Secrets of a Successful Life* (South Plainfield: Bridge Publishing, 1983), 87.

10 Dr. Richard J. Krejcir, "Statistics and Reasons for Church Decline," http://www.intothyword.org/articles_view.asp?articleid=36557, accessed June 11, 2013.

11 Krejcir, *Statistics.*

12 Krejcir, *Statistics.*

13 George Hunter III, *How to Reach Secular People.* (Nashville: Abingdon Press, 1992), 35.

14 Dr. Donald Soper, "Outlines for Christians' Witness Plans," in *The Methodist Recorder*, Jan. 15,1953. Dr. Soper says that a reasonable presentation of Christianity must come before the appeal, and must not be viewed as a minor stage in the process.

15 Allan Walker, *The Whole Gospel for the Whole World.* (Nashville: Abingdon Press, 1961), 29-30.

16 D. Michael Martin, *1, 2 Thessalonians, The New American Commentary*, vol. 33, (Nashville: Broadman & Holman Publishers, 2001), 58. electronic ed., Logos Library System.

17 *Theological Dictionary of the New Testament*, ed. Gerhard Kittel, Geoffrey W. Bromiley and Gerhard Friedrich, (Grand Rapids: Eerdmans, 1964), electronic ed., 302. As the essence of God is power, so endowment with power is linked with the gift of His Spirit. Endowment with the Spirit gives Him ἐξουσία, a definite personal authority which He has, in substantial terms, the δύναμις to exercise.

18 William Arndt, Frederick W. Danker, and Walter Bauer, *A Greek-English Lexicon of the New Testament and Other Early Christian Literature.* (Chicago: University of Chicago Press, 2000), 262.

19 George Barna, "Most American Christians Do Not Believe that Satan or the Holy Spirit Exist,"http://www.barna.org/barna-update/article/12-faithspirituality/260-most-american-christians-do-not-believe-that-satan-or-the-holy-spirit-exist, accessed April 10, 2009.

20 Barna, "Most American Christians Do Not Believe that Satan or the Holy Spirit Exist."

21 The Corinthians loved public orations (Dio Chrysostom Or. 37.33). Paul saw the use of "the wisdom of rhetoric" (1 Cor. 1:17) as the means of "emptying" the preaching of the cross, for the sophist was more interested in the skillful structuring and delivery of a speech than in its content (Epictetus Diss. 3.23.23–25).

22 Raymond Edward Brown, Joseph A. Fitzmyer, and Roland Edmund Murphy, *The Jerome Biblical Commentary.* (Englewood Cliffs: Prentice-Hall, 1996), 2, 786.

23 Brown, *Jerome Biblical Commentary,* 787.

Chapter Five

Evangelizing the Lost in the New Testament

[F]or our gospel did not come to you in word only, but also in power and in the Holy Spirit and with full conviction; just as you know what kind of men we proved to be among you for your sake.

(1 Thessalonians 1:5)

The Spirit-filled life is not a special, deluxe edition of Christianity. It is part and parcel of the total plan of God for His people.

– A.W. Tozer

Have you ever read a scripture passage afterward said to yourself, "This is just too good to be true"? In John 14:12, Jesus said, "Truly, truly, I say to you, whoever believes in me will also do the works that I do; and greater works than these will he do, because I am going to the Father" (ESV). I used to think, after reading this passage, that it was prideful to think that I could do what Jesus did. The very idea of my doing any works that were greater than the works Jesus did seemed to me absurd at best, and at worst, sinfully presumptuous. Yet Jesus says clearly that the works He did we also shall do. Here's the critical question: "Was Jesus lying or did He mean what He said?" Was this simply Jesus' rhetoric or did He say it to encourage us to go after it?

Walter A. Elwell says of Jesus' teaching method:

Jesus was in every respect a master communicator. He employed methods that were sufficiently familiar to his hearers to make them comfortable but sufficiently different to arrest their attention. What struck them most forcefully of all, however, was the person himself—Jesus taught them as one having authority…At least three things combined to make Jesus' very presence an unsettling challenge, a call to decision. First and foremost, he embodied what he taught, and what he taught seemed clearly beyond human capacities. Yet he embodied those principles to the highest degree without any embarrassment or arrogance… Second, his teaching was derived solely from the Old Testament, which was, of course, God's Word, and it was mediated directly through himself; he identified directly with it. The rabbis found it necessary to bolster their interpretations by extensive references to one another. Jesus never quoted another rabbi. "You have heard it said, but I say unto you" is how Jesus taught. God's word and his own words merged into one. Third, Jesus' words were backed up by demonstrations of power. Anyone can claim anything, but only one with more than human authority can say to the waves "Be still" and have those waves obey him.[1]

Jesus proceeded through a deliberate period of preparation before initiating his personal ministry:

- He is baptized in the Jordan River by John the Baptist (Mt. 3:13-17)
- He fasts in the wilderness for 40 days, where he is tempted by Satan (Mt. 4:1-11)
- He launches his ministry in Galilee, preaching the message, "Repent, for the kingdom of heaven is at hand" (Mt. 4:12-17 ESV)
- He calls His first disciples—Peter, Andrew, James, and John, who were fishermen—and tells him, "Follow me, and I will make you fishers of men" (Mt. 4:18-22 ESV)

- He increases his ministry by teaching in the synagogues, proclaiming the gospel of the kingdom, and healing every disease and affliction of the people, resulting in the drawing of great crowds from a wide area (Mt. 4:23-25)

Here are a few highlights that illustrate the ways Jesus ministered to people (emphasis added in each):

*15 The woman said to Him, "Sir, give me this water, so I will not be thirsty nor come all the way here to draw." 16 He said to her, "Go, call your husband and come here." 17 The woman answered and said, "I have no husband." Jesus said to her, "You have correctly said, 'I have no husband'; 18 for you have had five husbands, and the one whom you now have is not your husband; this you have said truly." 19 **The woman said to Him, "Sir, I perceive that You are a prophet"** (John 4:15-19).*

*A large crowd followed Him, because **they saw the signs which He was performing on those who were sick** (John 6:2).*

*Therefore **when the people saw the sign** which He had performed, they said, "This is truly the Prophet who is to come into the world" (John 6:14).*

*23 Jesus was going throughout all Galilee, teaching in their synagogues and proclaiming the gospel of the kingdom, and **healing every kind of disease and every kind of sickness among the people.***

*24 **The news about Him spread** throughout all Syria; and they brought to Him all who were ill, those suffering with various diseases and pains, demoniacs, epileptics, paralytics; and He healed them. 25 **Large crowds followed Him** from Galilee and the Decapolis and Jerusalem and Judea and from beyond the Jordan. (Matthew 4:23–25).*

*5 These twelve Jesus sent out after instructing them: "Do not go in the way of the Gentiles, and do not enter any city of the Samaritans; 6 but rather go to the lost sheep of the house of Israel. 7 "And as you go, preach, saying, 'The kingdom of heaven is at hand.' 8 "**Heal** the **sick, raise** the **dead, cleanse** the **lepers, and cast out demons.** Freely you received, freely give (Matthew 10:5–8).*

When Jesus ministered to the woman at the well in John 4, He used a prophetic word to reveal himself to her.[2] John tells us that large crowds followed Him because they saw the signs that He was performing. Jesus' method of proclaiming the gospel and the kingdom of God utilized the prophetic along with the healing of all who were ill, all who were suffering from "diseases and pains, demoniacs, epileptics, [and] paralytics" (Mt. 4:24b). When He called the twelve together in Matthew 10, He gave them authority to do the same thing He was doing. He told them that the determining factor for the kingdom of God was to "[h]eal the sick, raise the dead, cleanse the lepers, and cast out demons" (Mt. 10:8a). This was Jesus' discipleship model. It's what He told His disciples to do, and they did it throughout the New Testament. Has His model changed, or have we changed His command to preach the gospel, heal the sick, raise the dead and cleanse the lepers?

Jesus models for us what we are to do; a disciple does what the master teacher does. Jesus delegated His authority to us, and modeled for us how to reach the lost. James addressed this when he wrote, "But be doers of the word, and not hearers only, deceiving yourselves" (Ja. 1:22 ESV). There are two types of responses when we hear Jesus speak: we will be either hearers or doers. Doers act upon what they hear. Hearers don't act upon what they hear because the reality is that they don't really believe it or have a conviction to act upon it. James says that those who are hearers only are deceived. To be deceived means to be misled or deluded. In other words, don't kid yourself or lie to yourself; if you are a hearer and not a doer, you are deceived; you are not walking in kingdom reality. So, the tension of this deception can be a kingdom issue: Are we more concerned with Jesus' kingdom and serving the King, or are we deluded into seeking the approval of men and this world?

The apostle Paul was under no such delusion; he was sold out completely to Jesus Christ. That is why he was so effective evangelizing Gentiles, especially in the large cities of Asia Minor and southern Europe. If you happen to live in a large city, you may easily relate to Paul in his urban ministry as he regularly confronted gross debauchery in the cities. Corinth was such a place, a major seaport with a reputation in the ethics and morality departments that was sketchy, to say the least. Corinth's decadence was legendary, even in a Roman Empire that was itself known for its decadence. Paul certainly had his work cut out for him, but he was not intimidated. Instead, his example shows us how to invade an unbelieving culture with the gospel.

When Paul came to Corinth, he entered a culture well familiar with rhetorical speeches, occult healings, and prophecies. But Paul took a different approach. As Alan Johnson observes, "But did Paul use a rhetorical style at Corinth? The answer is clearly no, if by 'rhetorical style' we mean a cleverly devised presentation designed to emotionally move people to Paul's point of view and ultimately to praise him as a high-status rhetoric."[3] Corinth was home to a temple dedicated to Asclepius, the god of healing, and his daughter, Hygeia. Patients traveled there from all over the world to find healing.[4] The oracle of the shrine of Apollo at Delphi also was familiar to the Corinthian culture.[5] How, then, did Paul evangelize a culture accustomed to great orators, occult healings, and prophetic utterances? In his own words, "[A]nd my message and my preaching were not in persuasive words of wisdom, but in demonstration of the Spirit and of power [*dunamis*], so that your faith would not rest on the wisdom of men, but on the power [*dunamis*] of God" (1 Cor. 2:4–5).

Paul stressed to his readers that his message and preaching were not in words of human wisdom (*sophia* σοφία), but in demonstration of spirit and power (*dunamis* δύναμις) that would be a convincing proof for them.[6] Paul did not rely on his own abilities to preach, but on God's power, the same power by which Jesus validated His gospel message. John Chrysostom, an early church father, had this to say about 1 Cor.2:4:

> Now if the doctrine preached had nothing subtle, and they that were called were unlearned, and he that preached was of the same description,

43

and thereto was added persecution, and trembling, and fear; tell me, how did they overcome without Divine power? And this is why, having said, My speech and my preaching was not in persuasive words of wisdom, he added, but in demonstration of the Spirit and of power. Dost thou perceive how 'the foolishness of God is wiser than men, and the weakness stronger?' They for their part, being unlearned and preaching such a Gospel, in their chains and persecution overcame their persecutors. Whereby? Was it not by their furnishing that evidence which is of the Spirit? For this indeed is confessed demonstration. For who, tell me, after he had seen dead men rising to life and devils cast out, could have helped admitting it?[7]

For Chrysostom, the convincing evidence behind Paul's words was that dead men were raised back to life and devils were cast out of those who were possessed, not that some radically gifted preacher delivered an amazing sermon on YouTube with crazy visuals and a high-decibel worship team backing him up. The evidence that captured the heart of the Corinthian church was the demonstration of God's power. They saw it, they witnessed it, and it became reality to them. It was neither rhetoric nor a cleverly devised gospel presentation. Clearly, the early church's paradigm for the evidence of the truth of the gospel message was the revealing of the Holy Spirit in power to non-Christ followers. People who had never experienced God before now did. This is a great apologetic for the metamodernist: they felt it, they saw it, and then they believed it.

> [10] *Therefore I am well content with weaknesses, with insults, with distresses, with persecutions, with difficulties, for Christ's sake; for when I am weak, then I am strong.* [11] *I have become foolish; you yourselves compelled me. Actually, I should have been commended by you, for in no respect was I inferior to the most eminent apostles, even though I am a nobody.* [12] *The signs of a true apostle were performed among you with all perseverance, by signs and wonders and miracles* (2 Corinthians 12:10–12).

Paul established his position as an apostle by signs, wonders, and miracles. He assumed the role of apostle by his stated weakness, perseverance, signs, wonders, and miracles as a validation of a true apostle. Hawthorne says, "Paul's testimony is that miracles occurred wherever he proclaimed the good news and those remained essential to the life of the church."[8] He goes on to say, "'signs and wonders' were the miracles he performed empowered by the Spirit and integrally associated with his preaching to form part of the new Exodus to the freedom possible in the age of Christ. Thus, the gospel is, in part, the miracles that were performed (cf. Rom.15:18–19; 1 Th. 1:5)"[9] and the spoken word. According to Paul's paradigm of ministry, miracles are needed to prove the gospel message; they validate the gospel of Jesus' kingdom. Miracles would lead people to Christ and then Paul would explain in his letters (such as Romans) how to grow in this new faith.

> [16]*to be a minister of Christ Jesus to the Gentiles, ministering as a priest the gospel of God, so that* my *offering of the Gentiles may become acceptable, sanctified by the Holy Spirit.* [17]*Therefore in Christ Jesus I have found reason for boasting in things pertaining to God.* [18]*For I will not presume to speak of anything except what Christ has accomplished through me, resulting in the obedience of the Gentiles by word and deed,* [19]*in the power of signs and wonders, in the power of the Spirit; so that from Jerusalem and round about as far as Illyricum I have fully preached the gospel of Christ.* [20] *And thus I aspired to preach the gospel, not where Christ was* already *named, so that I would not build on another man's foundation* (Romans 15:16–20).

Again, Paul does not rely on his years of education or his positional authority when entering new ministry areas, but only on "the power of signs and wonders, in the power of the Spirit" as he communicates the gospel to the Gentiles. A powerless gospel would be irrelevant to the Gentiles. Thus, the *modus operandi* for proclaiming the gospel and the validation of his apostleship were based solely on the power of signs, wonders, and power in the Spirit. It was an indisputable apologetic for them.

I have seen some pretty crazy stuff in my own life. Once, I was in a meeting with a guy named Mahesh Chavda, and as he spoke, all of a sudden the room started to smell like roses. I had no idea what was going on, but the lady next to me started crying out, "He is the Rose of Sharon." I will never forget that, but I am not sure I got it. Signs point the way to Jesus. He is the Rose of Sharon. I might not have understood the sign, but all such signs should point us to Him. That happened about thirty years ago, and today I get it; the smell of roses pointed to the fact that He was in the room with us that day. The Greek word behind the English *signs* is σημεῖον, occurring 73 times in the New Testament.[10] Rengstorf remarks that it "is less a sign than an indication or pointer."[11] It is the sign or distinguishing mark by which something is known.[12] Danker defines it as "an event that is an indication or confirmation of intervention by transcendent powers." Luke 2:12 illustrates this, while foreshadowing the cross.[13] Therefore, signs point the way to the cross; they prove the validity of the gospel message. It's kind of like the football player in the Tom Cruise movie *Jerry McGuire*, who says, "Show me the money." Paul showed them the "money"—the power of God by a sign. Perhaps you have received a weird sign that you are not sure about. The best way to determine if it is a God sign or not is to ask the question, "Did it point me to Jesus?"

The purpose for wonders is nicely illustrated in Exodus 4:21: "The LORD said to Moses, 'When you go back to Egypt see that you perform before Pharaoh all the wonders which I have put in your power; but I will harden his heart so that he will not let the people go.'" Kittel's *Theological Dictionary* says this about wonders: "Something which discloses what He can do."[14] This picture receives some correspondence and confirmation as it finds repetition in the way that the early Christians speak of the miracles of the apostolic age. Wonders leave you amazed at Jesus; you cannot help but wonder at how great He is.

Ignatius, martyred in AD 117 by Trajan, in a comment on Exodus 4:21, remarks, "He also lived a holy life, and healed every kind of sickness and disease among the people, and wrought signs and wonders for the benefit of men; and to those who had fallen into the error of polytheism."[15]

In other words, the purpose of Moses' miracles and signs was to validate that there is only one true God; Moses' miracles pointed to and proved the power of God to a skeptical Pharaoh and his court.

Origen of Alexandria (185-254 CE) points out how Exodus 4:21 presaged Jesus:

> And as it was necessary, in order that Moses should find credit not only among the elders, but the common people, that there should be performed those miracles which he is recorded to have performed, why should not Jesus also, in order that He may be believed on by those of the people who had learned to ask for signs and wonders, need to work such miracles as, on account of their greater grandeur and divinity (in comparison with those of Moses), were able to convert men from Jewish fables, and from the human traditions which prevailed among them, and make them admit that He who taught and did such things was greater than the prophets? For how was He not greater than the prophets, who was proclaimed by them to be the Christ, and the Savior of the human race?[16]

For Origen, signs and wonders gave credibility to the one delivering the message, making him believable. Signs and wonders encourage people to believe and say that Jesus is greater than any before Him.

Gregory Thaumaturgus (his name means "the miracle worker," he lived 213-270 years after the death of Christ) had the power to heal by the laying on of his hands. Often, the healing was so powerful that the patient, cured of his illness, became a fervent convert on the spot.[17] Gregory explained his use of signs, wonders, and miracles as found in the book of Romans:

> I pray I may glory through Jesus Christ in those things, which pertain to God. **For I dare not to speak of any of those things which Christ**

hath not wrought by me, to make the Gentiles obedient, by word and deed, through mighty signs and wonders, by the power of the Holy Spirit. And again: Now I beseech you, brethren, for our Lord Jesus Christ's sake, and by the love of the Spirit. And these things, indeed, are written in the Epistle to the Romans (emphasis added).[18]

It is noted that when Gregory died there were only seventeen non-Christians in his town.[19] Gregory came into a culture that did not know the stories. He used signs, wonders, and miracles as an apologetic for the legitimacy of Christ's power. He led virtually an entire town to the Lord by demonstrating the power of God to an unbelieving people.

Yale professor Ramsay McMullen writes, "Of all worships, the Christian best and most particularly advertised its miracles by driving out of spirits and laying on of hands. Reports would spread without need of preaching."[20] Gregory and the other early church fathers grasped the need for a demonstration of the power of God. When one's son is healed, the propensity for the family's conversion is high. They might not know the story, but they have just encountered a God who is more powerful than the gods they have been serving.

Regarding the Roman culture in the time of early church fathers, McMullen says, "Theirs (the Christian) is truly a God all-powerful. He has worked a hundred wonders…great is the God of the Christians."[21] This was the apologetic of the early church, to proclaim the gospel not only in words but also in divine power. In other words, the proof is in the pudding. The proof is in what you see and taste, not in reading the directions.

This is how the apostles and early church demonstrated the gospel to the lost.

The Book of Acts shows us how the early church operated and functioned. Some say that the Book of Acts should be a model or prescriptive of how we are to do church while others feel it is just descriptive of the first-century church.[22] It wasn't just the apostles who were doing this stuff; the body of Christ as a whole was doing it. They were doing what they saw Jesus, and then the apostles, do. As a first-century model of discipleship it went something like: "You watch while I do, and then you do and have others watch and then do." They were doing the stuff in the Book of Acts, proving the reality of Christ to a lost world. Could it be, perhaps, that we don't see this a lot in America because our leaders don't model it for us?

> **Even Simon himself believed**; and after being baptized, he continued on with Philip, and **as he observed signs and great miracles taking place, he was constantly amazed** (Acts 8:13, emphasis added).

Acts does not tell us much about Simon except that he was powerful in the eyes of the Samaritans. Later church lore regards him as the founder of Gnosticism, leading many astray with his sect the *Simonians* (Irenaeus, *Against Heresies* 1.23).[23] Simon observed signs and wonders greater than he was capable of doing. The extracanonical Apocryphal Acts of Peter (2nd-3rd century A.D.[24]) describes a meeting between Simon and Peter in Rome:

> Later, there was a conflict with Simon in the forum in the presence of the senators and prefects. First the combatants exchanged words; then the contest switched, and the power of Peter was signally exhibited as greater than Simon's in raising the dead. Simon was now discredited in Rome, and in a last attempt to recover his influence he declared that he would ascend to God. Before the assembled crowd he flew up over the city, but in answer to Peter's prayer to Christ he fell down and broke his leg in three places. He was removed from Rome and, after having his leg amputated, died.[25]

The Book of Acts and ancient tradition inform us that Simon knew magical powers, but because they did not compare to Peter's, he wanted to purchase that power from Peter. Such power was visible and appealing to the nonbeliever.

When I was pastoring in Northern California, I once led a woman to the Lord who told me that she had a daughter who was a Wiccan practitioner. She asked me if I would pray for her. Of course, I told her, "No problem, I'll do that." We lived in the foothills of Northern California and I had to drive up the mountain. As I was driving up it started to snow, but I was praying, "Jesus, what am I going to say to this girl?" When I got there, I was led out to their redwood deck in the back yard. She brought her daughter out to me. She was dressed all in black, including black lipstick and black-painted finger nails, and wearing pentagram earrings and a big pentagram pendant. What are you supposed to say to a person like that? "Nice pentagram ear rings; did you get that at the Wiccan section in Walmart"?

Her name was Shawnee. I told her, "Shawnee, obviously I came here to talk about spiritual things with you. This is what the Lord told me about you: He said that when you were four years old you received Him into your life."

"So what?"

"Strike one," I thought. Then I went on. "He told me that you were in a near-fatal car wreck but were spared any injury."

"So what?"

Wow, strike two for me. Then I said, "You have never told anyone one this, but when you were 16 your youth pastor tried to put a sexual move on you. You were so disgusted by this that you told yourself you would never go to church again."

Even as I said this, her eyes were tearing up. "You're right," she said, "I have never told anyone that before." She and I both were amazed at how God met her like this.

As we were finishing up, I figured I would do a "Wiccan-sensitive" prayer (not that I know what that is) and said, "Jesus, you created everything in this forest for Shawnee. You created the birds in the forest to sing for her." By this time it was snowing harder, a heavy, wet snow with big flakes falling, and the forest was really quiet. Just as finished my prayer, it seemed suddenly as if all the birds in the forest started chirping, squawking, and bellowing loudly all at once. I thought to myself, "I guess I am the 'bird whisperer' or something." I then said aloud, "Jesus, you even made the sun to shine upon her face." At that moment, instantly, the clouds cleared and a beam of light came out of the sky and shined upon us for an instant. The temperature also went up instantly to where we both took a step back. Then I said something really spiritual like, "Oh, my God!" I had goose bumps on my arm, and when I looked at Shawnee, I saw that she was just as amazed as I.

She came to church the following Sunday and said, "Do you notice anything different about me?"

Not knowing what to say at first, I finally said, "Thanks for not wearing your pentagram earrings to church."

"No," she said, "that's not it. I am a follower of Jesus now."

Signs and wonders led people to Jesus in the early church and it still happens today. You just have to be willing to take the risk, and that can involve rejection. Hey, news flash: if they rejected Jesus, they may reject you as well; that's the way of the cross (Lk. 9:23).

We see this model of ministering in power all throughout the Book of Acts: the use of signs and wonders following the proclamation of the gospel. For example: "Therefore they spent a long time *there* speaking boldly *with reliance* upon the Lord, who was testifying to the word of His grace, granting that signs and wonders be done by their hands" (Acts 14:3).

The word for testifying (μαρτυρέω) has the primary meaning of "bear witness;" testify to the truth by personal knowledge.[26] Shawnee, the Wiccan girl, had a personal knowledge that God is real because she experienced a power greater than she had ever witnessed before. Again, the primary vehicle that the disciples used to convey the truth of the gospel was to perform signs and wonders through the laying on of their hands. This gave an understanding (revelation) to the unbeliever that the message of the disciples was true. Signs and wonders were a validating truth for the apostles. It was their primary vehicle for confirming the truth of the gospel message to an unbelieving audience.

[11]God was performing extraordinary miracles by the hands of Paul, [12]so that handkerchiefs or aprons were even carried from his body to the sick, and the diseases left them and the evil spirits went out. [13]But also some of the Jewish exorcists, who went from place to place, attempted to name over those who had the evil spirits the name of the Lord Jesus, saying, 'I adjure you by Jesus whom Paul preaches.' [14]Seven sons of one Sceva, a Jewish chief priest, were doing this. [15]And the evil spirit answered and said to them, 'I recognize Jesus, and I know about Paul, but who are you?[16]And the man, in whom was the evil spirit, leaped on them and subdued all of them and overpowered them, so that they fled out of that house naked and wounded. [17]This became known to all, both Jews and Greeks, who lived in Ephesus; and fear fell upon them all and the name of the Lord Jesus was being magnified. [18]Many also of those who had believed kept coming, confessing and disclosing their practices. [19]And many of those who practiced magic brought their books together and began burning them in the sight of everyone; and they counted up the price of them and found it fifty thousand pieces of silver. [20]So the word of the Lord was growing mightily and prevailing (Acts 19:11-20).

The miracles performed by Paul ranged from ordinary miracles to extraordinary works of power. Healing the lame (Acts 3:11, 14:8), exorcism (Acts 16:18), and confronting a sorcerer (Acts 13:6-10) were ordinary miracles for Paul. Now Paul released *dunamis* (δύναμις) into objects that could be given to people to heal their sicknesses and diseases and to exorcise demons. As with Simon Magus, the sons of Sceva saw this and thought they could use it as a formula for their exorcisms. Instead, the demon turned on them. How ironic that a revelation to Paul by the Holy Spirit was perceived as a method to the sons of Sceva, leading to a ritual, which proved ineffective against demonic powers. Because of Paul's ministry of power, many confessed Christ, disclosed their sins, repented, and burned their expensive occult books.

Notes

1   Walter A. Elwell, ed., *Baker Theological Dictionary of the Bible*. (Grand Rapids: Baker Books, a division of Baker Book House Company, 1996), 401.

2   First Corinthians14:25 says that prophecy is the secrets of one's heart being revealed. Here, Jesus is operating in that gift.

3   Alan F. Johnson, *First Corinthians, The IVP New Testament Commentary*. (Downers Grove: InterVarsity Press, 2004), 27.

4   Jack Finegan, *Corinth*. (Louisville: Review and Expositor, 1980), 317.

5   Charles R. Smith, *Grace Theological Journal Volume vol. 10, No 2*. (Winona Lake: Grace Seminary, 1989), 23.

6   James Swanson, *Dictionary of Biblical Languages with Semantic Domains: Greek (New Testament)*, (Oak Harbor: Logos Research Systems, Inc., 1997), electronic ed.

7   John Chrysostom, "Homilies of St. John Chrysostom, Archbishop of Constantinople, on the First Epistle of St. Paul the Apostle to the Corinthians," trans. Hubert Kestell Cornish, John Medley, and Talbot B. Chambers, in *A Select Library of the Nicene and Post-Nicene Fathers of the Christian Church, First Series, Volume XII: Saint Chrysostom: Homilies on the Epistles of Paul to the Corinthians*, ed. Philip Schaff (New York: Christian Literature Company, 1889), 30.

8   Gerald F. Hawthorne, Ralph P. Martin, and Daniel G. Reid, *Dictionary of Paul and His Letters* (Downers Grove: InterVarsity Press, 1993), 875.

9   Hawthorne, *Dictionary*, 875.

10 Karl Rengstorf, *Theological Dictionary of the New Testament*, vol. VII, ed. Gerhard Kittel, Geoffrey W. Bromiley and Gerhard Friedrich, (Grand Rapids: Wm. B. Eerdmans, 1964), 229, electronic ed.

11 Rengstorf, *Theological Dictionary of the New Testament*, VII, 202.

12 William Arndt, et al., *A Greek-English Lexicon of the New Testament and Other Early Christian Literature : a Translation and Adaption of the Fourth Revised and Augmented Edition of Walter Bauer's Griechisch-deutsches Worterbuch Zu Den Schrift En Des Neuen Testaments Und Der Ubrigen Urchristlichen Literatur*. (Chicago: University of Chicago Press, 1979), 747.

13 Rengstorf, *Theological Dictionary of the New Testament*, VII, 231.

14 Gerhard Kittel, Geoffrey W. Bromiley, and Gerhard Friedrich, eds., *Theological Dictionary of the New Testament* (Grand Rapids: Wm. B. Eerdmans, 1964), 124–125.

15 Ignatius of Antioch, "The Epistle of Ignatius to the Magnesians" in *The An-te-Nicene Fathers, Volume I: The Apostolic Fathers with Justin Martyr and Irenae-us*, eds. Alexander Roberts, James Donaldson and A. Cleveland Coxe, (Buffalo: Christian Literature Company, 1885), 64.

16 Origen, "Origen Against Celsus," trans. Frederick Crombie, in *The An-te-Nicene Fathers, Volume IV: Fathers of the Third Century: Tertullian, Part Fourth; Minucius Felix; Commodian; Origen, Parts First and Second*, Alexander Roberts, James Donaldson, and A. Cleveland Coxe, eds. (Buffalo: Christian Literature Company, 1885), 452.

17 "Saint Gregory Thaumaturgus," http://saints.sqpn.com/saintg40.htm, accessed June 11, 2013. Saint Gregory Thaumaturgus was a noted miracle worker who moved rivers and performed numerous other miracles.

18 "Pseudo-Gregory Thaumaturgus, A Sectional Confession of Faith", trans. S. D. F. Salmond, in *The Ante-Nicene Fathers, Volume VI: Fathers of the Third Century: Gregory Thaumaturgus, Dionysius the Great, Julius Africanus, Anatolius and Minor Writers, Methodius, Arnobius*, Alexander Roberts, James Donaldson, and A. Cleveland Coxe, eds. (Buffalo: Christian Literature Company, 1886), 43.

19 http://www.catholic.org/saints/saint.php?saint_id=656, accessed 6/11/2013.

20 Ramsay McMullen, *Christianizing The Roman Empire A.D. 100-400.* (New Haven: Yale University Press,1984) 40.

21 McMullen, *Christianizing The Roman Empire*, 41.

22 John R. W. Stott, *Baptism and Fullness.* (Downers Grove: InterVarsity Press, 1975), 15-17. "**What is described in Scripture as having happened to others is not necessarily intended for us**, whereas what is promised to us we should appropriate, and what is commanded us we are to obey…What is descriptive is valuable (in determining what God intends for all Christians) only in so far as it is interpreted by what is didactic…**We must derive our standards of belief and behavior from the teaching of the New Testament**…rather than from the practices and experiences which it portrays" (emphasis added). Jesus told His disciples to lay hands on the sick and they would recover. Paul tells us to earnestly desire spiritual gifts. James tells us to lay hands on the sick. Is this descriptive or prescriptive?

23 Chalmer Ernest Faw, *Acts: Believers Church Bible Commentary* (Scottdale: Herald Press, 1993), 104.

24 Geoffrey W. Bromiley, ed., *The International Standard Bible Encyclopedia, Revised.* (Grand Rapids: Wm. B. Eerdmans, 1988, 2002), 1165.

25 Geoffrey W. Bromiley, *The International Standard Bible Dictionary*, 1170. "One of the earliest of the apocryphal acts of the apostles, the Acts of Peter reports a

miracle contest between Simon Magus and the apostle Peter in Rome. It con-
cludes with Peter's martyrdom. The Acts of Peter was originally composed in
Greek during the second half of the 2d century, probably in Asia Minor. The
majority of the text has survived only in the Latin translation of the Vercelli
manuscript. The concluding chapters are preserved separately as the Martyrdom of Peter in three Greek manuscripts and in Coptic (fragmentary), Syri-
ac, Ethiopic, Arabic, Armenian, and Slavonic versions." Robert F. Stoops Jr.,
"Peter, Acts Of," David Noel Freedman, ed., *The Anchor Yale Bible Dictionary.*
(New York: Doubleday, 1992), 267.

26 *A Greek-English Lexicon of the New Testament and Other Early Christian Literature, (BDAG)*, 3rd ed. (Chicago: University of Chicago Press, 2001), 617

Chapter Six

Normal People Can Do the Miraculous

I once was teaching a group of pastors how to move in the gifts of the Spirit when one of them interrupted me and said, "Well, only you can do this; we cannot." By the end of that meeting we had witnessed several people being healed, and it was those pastors who did it, not me. There is a tragic misconception in much of the body of Christ today that only certain people can operate in the miraculous. My Bible says that we are His elect. That means He hand-picked us—you—for this. That's how much you mean to God. To put it another way, if God had a refrigerator, your picture would be on it (Eph. 2:20).

Some Bible scholars insist that only the apostles could to the miraculous workings of Christ. Yet, the New Testament clearly depicts non-apostles—ordinary people—also performing miracles, signs, and wonders just as the twelve did.:

And Stephen, full of grace and power, was performing great wonders and signs among the people (Acts 6:8).

⁵Philip went down to the city of Samaria and began *proclaiming Christ to them. ⁶The crowds with one accord were giving attention to what was said by Philip, as they heard and saw the signs which he was performing. ⁷For* in the case of *many who had unclean spirits, they were coming out* of them *shouting with a loud voice; and many who had been paralyzed and lame were healed* (Acts 8:5–7).

Even Simon himself believed; and after being baptized, he continued on with Philip, and as he observed signs and great miracles taking place, he was constantly amazed (Acts 8:13).

[11]And the Lord said to him, "Get up and go to the street called Straight, and inquire at the house of Judas for a man from Tarsus named Saul, for he is praying, [12] and he has seen in a vision a man named Ananias come in and lay his hands on him, so that he might regain his sight" (Acts 9:11–12).

One of them named Agabus stood up and began to indicate by the Spirit that there would certainly be a great famine all over the world. And this took place in the reign of Claudius (Acts 11:28).

The things you have learned and received and heard and seen in me, practice these things, and the God of peace will be with you (Philippians 4:9).

Professor G.W.H. Lampe of Cambridge says the following of Stephen, Phillip, and Ananias:[1]

Stephen's own preaching was accompanied, like that of the apostles, by signs and wonders done publicly (6, 8)...so, too with Philip at Samaria: the word is associated with works, exorcisms, and the healing of the paralyzed and the lame, which recall the acts of Jesus as prophesied in Isaiah 35 (Isa.35:5-6) and which are described as 'signs' (Acts 8:6, 13)...In the story of the conversion of Saul,...the enemy of the gospel is struck down and blinded by the power of God...He is restored to sight...by Ananias, who, in fulfilling this commission, is acting as the direct agent of Jesus.[2]

The *Wycliffe Bible Encyclopedia* says of Agabus:

A prophet from Jerusalem (Acts 11:27-30) who predicted a worldwide famine in the inhabited world (the Roman Empire). This occurred in the days of Claudius (A.D. 41-54), relief being sent probably between the years 45-46 by the Antioch church in Syria to the Jerusalem Christians. Presumably, the same Agabus is intended in Acts 21:10, 11, where his prediction made in A.D. 59 to the church at Caesarea was dramatically presented by his binding himself with Paul's girdle, warning Paul of impending imprisonment if he insisted on going up to Jerusalem.[3]

Not only did non-apostles perform miracles, but Paul also encouraged people to imitate him as he imitated Christ (1 Cor. 11:1; Phil. 4:9). He told them to practice the things that they saw him do, referring to miracles, signs, and wonders. Practice (πράσσω) means to bring about or accomplish something through activity.[4] He leaves them with a charge to continue what he did; they need to rehearse, or put into use, the *dunamis* of God. It implies that they might not get it right immediately, but given time, with the gift of miracles, signs, and wonders, you will win the lost.

Wayne Grundmann states, "The history of Jesus is the history of the Christ because the kingdom of God comes with Him."[5] What then is this kingdom? In Luke 4:18, Jesus comes into the synagogue and pronounces his Messianic assignment, saying, "The Spirit of the Lord is upon me, because He anointed me to preach the gospel to the poor. He has sent me to proclaim release to the captives, And recovery of sight to the blind, to set free those who are oppressed." Jesus establishes His kingdom by preaching, releasing captives from their bondages, healing the blind, and setting the oppressed free. His ministry establishes the kingdom in order that the works of the devil (Jn. 10:10) may be abolished on earth as they are in heaven (Mt. 6:10).

In Matthew 4:17, Jesus comes out of the wilderness after forty days of fasting and confrontation with the devil. The devil departs from Him and Jesus makes the proclamation, "Repent, for the kingdom of heaven is at hand." A kingdom is the place where a king has his domain; in his kingdom the king is the sovereign ruler. Matthew wrote, "Jesus was going throughout all Galilee, teaching in their synagogues and proclaiming the gospel of the kingdom, and healing every kind of disease and every kind of sickness among the people" (Mt. 4:23). We see that the gospel of Jesus' kingdom is established on earth by the healing of disease and sickness, thus abolishing the works of Satan, which bring sickness, disease, bondage, and oppression. Jesus' kingdom is also established by the elimination of demonic holds upon man (1 Jn. 3:8). Jesus gave his disciples authority over unclean spirits, to cast them out, and to heal every kind of disease and every kind of sickness (Mt. 10:1). If we wish to demonstrate the King and His kingdom, we should expect to operate the way Jesus instructed His disciples: "And as you go, preach, saying, 'The kingdom of heaven is at hand.' "Heal *the* sick, raise *the* dead, cleanse *the* lepers, cast out demons. Freely you received, freely give" (Mt. 10:7-8). Jesus' form of evangelism presented a triumphant kingdom that had dominion over the sick and the demonized.

Notes

1   E. E. Ellis, *Prophecy and Hermeneutic in Early Christianity: New Testament Essays.* Wissenschaftliche Untersuchungen zum Neuen Testament, vol.18. (Tubingen: J.C.B. Mohr (Paul Siebeck). See the similar remarks of Cyril H. Powell, *The Biblical Concept of Power.* (London: Epworth Press, 1963), 139, 143.

2   G. W. H. Lampe, in C. F. D. Moule, ed., *Miracles: Cambridge Studies in Their Philosophy and History.* (London: A. R. Mowbray & Co. Ltd., 1966), 175-76.

3   Charles F. Pfeiffer, Howard Frederic Vos, and John Rea, *The Wycliffe Bible Encyclopedia.* (Chicago: Moody Press, 1975; 2005).

4   *BDAG*, 861.

5   Grundmann, *Theological Dictionary of the New Testament*, 2, 302. Power is one of God's attributes, so endowment with power is linked with the gift of His Spirit. Endowment with the Spirit gives Him ἐξουσία, a definite personal authority which He has, in substantial terms, the δύναμις to exercise.

Chapter Seven

Evidence of Post-Apostolic Era Charismata in the Church

Did the charismata, or gifts of the Spirit end with the apostolic age, as the cessationists contend, or did they continue to manifest and be used in the post-apostolic church? Documentary evidence clearly indicates that the charismata continued to appear in the early church even after the passing of the apostles. It is evident in the writings of the early Church Fathers that the power of God via spiritual gifts continued as an essential part in the proclamation and validation of the gospel message. As in New Testament times, the early Church Fathers both witnessed, and in many cases performed miracles by the power of the Spirit to prove the validity of Christ to the lost. For this reason, he thought that the charismata might come to an end never occurred to them.

As Eusebius A. Stephanou notes,

> Never did the Fathers, doctors, and other Christian writers express the view that the charismata belonged to an earlier age, were later withdrawn, and were not necessary for the church of subsequent ages. In my studies of patristic literature nowhere have I found the charismata rejected, disparaged, or prohibited. On the contrary, the charismatic nature of the church is universally acknowledged and proclaimed, always with direct references to the word of scripture.[1]

John, the last of apostles, died in approximately 100 A.D. If cessationism is correct, we should have no historical record of the charismata continuing. Such is not the case, however. The historical record, in fact, is replete with evidence demonstrating that, rather than ceasing, the gifts of the Spirit continued on in the life and ministry of the church.

The Didache is one of the church's earliest extant documents, dating from the late 1st or early 2nd century. It is an "operations manual" of sorts that, among other things, gives directions to the early church on how to treat prophets and apostles. In particular, the church is to actively support genuine prophets and teachers who take up residence with the people. *The Didache* says that the church members are to give the firstfruits of their produce to any prophets who are living among them (Did. 13.1-7). It makes no mention of the apostles appointing bishops and deacons; rather, the congregation as a whole are told to appoint for themselves worthy men as bishops and deacons. Once appointed, they are not to be despised, because they minister to the people the ministry of prophets and teachers (Did. 15.1-2).[2]

The Didache says, "Now concerning the apostles and prophets, deal with them as follows...Let every apostle who comes to you be welcomed as if he were the Lord. But he is not to stay for more than one day, unless there is need, in which case he may stay another. But if he stays three days, he is a false prophet."[3] If there were no longer prophets and apostles in the 2nd century, why would there be any need for such an instruction on how to discern and treat true prophets?[4] Apparently, there were enough prophets and apostles traveling at this time for guidelines to be needed.

The *Shepherd of Hermas,* which had near-canonical status in some sectors of the early church (e.g., Irenaeus), recounts many spiritual experiences.[5] Writing from Rome sometime in the 2nd century, the anonymous author of *Hermas* lists his own experiences with the charismata, including visions, angelic visitations, and voices from heaven. Compared with the *Didache, Hermas* presents more detailed archetypes of the true and false prophet. Naturally, the prophet's conduct was the clearest signal of his authenticity:

"How then, Sir," say I, "will a man know which of them is the prophet, and which the false prophet?" "I will tell you," says he, "about both the prophets, and then you can try the true and the false prophet according to my directions. Try the man who has the Divine Spirit by his life. The true prophet is tranquil, self-effacing, abstaining from evil and vain desire."

The Shepherd of Hermas paints a striking picture of the prophet's role in the church: Prophecy is not a clandestine event, but occurs when the Christian assembly prays and God decides to give a message. True prophets never take money for their messages. Because God obstructs the attempts of false prophets, these people find themselves unable to feign prophecy before the assembled church. Instead, individuals come to consult them and offer payment. False prophets give empty predictions, designed to gratify the desires of the supplicant. They are moved by an earthly spirit or even the devil himself and may damage the unstable Christian.[6]

The author of *Hermas* was noted for having angelic visitations and revelations on a regular basis. In one account, he relates, "After I had been praying at home, and had sat down on my couch, there entered a man of glorious aspect, dressed like a shepherd, with a white goat's skin, a wallet on his shoulders, and a rod in his hand, and saluted me. I returned his salutation. And straightway he sat down beside me, and said to me, 'I have been sent by a most venerable angel to dwell with you the remaining days of your life.'"[7]

Irenaeus (120-200 A.D.), a disciple of Polycarp, who was a disciple of John, wrote that the casting out of devils, healing, prophecy, and raising people from the dead were still occurring during his lifetime:

> For some do certainly and truly drive out devils, so that those who have thus been cleansed from evil spirits frequently both believe [in Christ], and join themselves to the Church. Others have foreknowledge of things to come: they see visions, and utter prophetic expressions.

Others still, heal the sick by laying their hands upon them, and they are made whole. Yea, moreover, as I have said, the dead even have been raised up, and remained among us for many years. And what shall I more say? It is not possible to name the number of the gifts which the Church, [scattered] throughout the whole world, has received from God, in the name of Jesus Christ, who was crucified under Pontius Pilate, and which she exerts day by day for the benefit of the Gentiles, neither practicing deception upon any, nor taking any reward from them [on account of such miraculous interpositions]. For as she has received freely from God, freely also does she minister [to others].[8]

Irenaeus says these gifts are for the benefit of the Gentiles. Thus, to Irenaeus, the most effective way to reach his generation was through the charismata, i.e., the prophetic, healing, and casting out of devils. These signs, validating the gospel message, would lead many pagan people to the Lord. Irenaeus carried on the model that Christ told his disciples to follow in Matthew 10:8, to heal the sick, raise the dead, and cleanse the leper.

Sozomen (400-450 A.D.), an early church historian, says that the early church fathers could effect miracles; he attested to having experienced them himself. He lists the miracles and those who performed them:

> For a demonstration of the same truth, miracles are wrought to effect physical cures, mental troubles, threatened dangers, casting out of demons, silencing philosophers and wordy ecclesiastics, vindicating orthodoxy, reading the thoughts of hypocrites, defeating enemies, sanctifying the sacraments, raising the dead; and they are the mighty agents for converting philosophers, Jews, pagans, and heretics. They are wrought by the hands of the eminently excellent only; the gift is associated with a high measure of grace; for example, the bishops Paphnutius (i. 10) and Spyridion (i. 11) are so endowed; Alexander of Constantinople (i. 14), Eusebius of Emesa (iii. 6), Martin of Tours (iii. 14), Arsacius of Nicomedia (iv. 16), Donatus (vii. 26), Gregory of Neocæsarea

(vii. 26), Theotimus of Scythia (vii. 26), Epiphanius of Salamis (vii. 27). In like manner, the monks Antony (i. 13), Amun (i. 14), Eutychianus (i. 14), Macarius the Egyptian, Apollonius, Hilarion, Julian (iii. 14), John, Copres, Helles, Apelles, Eulogius (vi. 28); Apollos, John of Diolchus, Benjamin and Pior (vi. 29).

Sozomen had a miracle produced upon him; he believed in an uninterrupted stream of the charismata, deeming them necessary for the preservation of the faith.[9] Far from denying the gifts, Sozomen plainly declared that they were still in effect in 400 A.D and were used to convert the unbelieving; the apologetic of power was still in effect.

Augustine (354-430 A.D.), early on in his ministry, advocated cessationism, but in his later writings retracted this stance. He had an ongoing experience of the miraculous, carefully documenting no fewer than seventy instances of divine healing in his own diocese during a two-year span (see *City of God*, Book XXII, 8-10). He also testified to seeing a blind man in Milan regaining his sight.[10]

Historically, we see that the gifts of the Spirit continued after the death of the last apostle. Biblically, we are commanded in 1 Corinthians 12-14 to be informed or aware of spiritual gifts, and in 1 Corinthians 14, are twice exhorted to earnestly desire spiritual gifts. Nowhere in the Bible is there any statement that declares that spiritual gifts, and especially the charismata, have ended; such a statement is just a theological denial of biblical truth. What is very clear is that we need to earnestly desire the gifts.

The Reformation of the 16th century brought about a knee-jerk reaction to any miracles performed in their times because of the Roman Catholic mindset which gave too much homage to the saints and to relics. In other words, the Catholic Church held to their position as the true church by the validation of the miraculous. How could one discredit someone whose claim to authenticity is the miraculous? That was one of the great challenges John Calvin had to overcome in his quest to legitimize the Reformation.

Calvin, the premier theologian of the Reformation, looked to the foundational principles of Christianity. In doing so, he delineated five distinctive doctrines, known as the "*sola*" (sole or alone) doctrines: *sola Scriptura*, by scripture alone; *sola Gratia*, by grace alone; *sola Fide*, by faith alone; *solus Christus*, by Christ alone; and *soli Deo Gloria*, glory to God alone. These fundamental tenets were designed to disempower the Roman Catholic Church's grip on Christendom. As Ruthven remarks, "If you are defending your doctrines, the last thing you want to do is concede miracle-working among your opponents."[11] Calvin and Luther believed that miracles existed only to prove correct doctrine and were not to be used to validate the kingdom of God to the unbelieving world.

The Reformers were, in general, skeptical of postbiblical miracles. Calvin in particular repudiates the claim that miracles continued in the Church to accredit the teaching of the Church. He denounced such works as "sheer delusions of Satan" that drew people away from God and should be repudiated in accordance with the teaching of Deut. 13; Mt. 24:24; and 2 Th. 2:9 (Inst., Prefatory Address; cf. also i.8.5–7; i.13.13; i.14.18; iv.19.6, 18). The miracles of scripture accredit the biblical revelation, which Calvin insisted is the test of all truth in religion. Miracles that draw people away from this do not bring glory to God in the way that the biblical miracles do. Hence, they must be rejected. The miracles of Christ show His divinity. They serve as sacramental signs, embodying in nature what God promises and does in His Word.[12]

Calvin regarded miracles as a means to validate the doctrine of *sola Scriptura*; therefore, scriptural truth becomes a correct doctrine. For Calvin, this apologetic of scripture alone became the crucible for tearing down the authority of the Catholic Church. In Calvin's view, miracles, except those stated in the Bible as revealing Christ's divinity, were delusions of Satan that drew people away from God. Thus, we see Calvin knee jerking in giving a non-biblical account for the purpose of miracles. In the Old Testament, was the miracle of Elisha praying that the eyes of his servant be opened demonstrating

Christ's divinity? In the New Testament, was the incident involving Ananias and Sapphira proving the divinity of Christ?

Calvin's logic was the same as that of the Pharisees, which Jesus rejects in Luke 11:17-20:

> [17]*But He knew their thoughts and said to them, "Any kingdom divided against itself is laid waste; and a house divided against itself falls. [18]If Satan also is divided against himself, how will his kingdom stand? For you say that I cast out demons by Beelzebul. [19]And if I by Beelzebul cast out demons, by whom do your sons cast them out? So they will be your judges. [20]But if I cast out demons by the finger of God, then the kingdom of God has come upon you."*

There is a correlation between the kingdom of God and his power being demonstrated. Calvin was incorrect in his perception of miracles; they are not to prove right doctrine but to show the kingdom of God to men. In the Protestant Reformation the focus of miracles changes; the Reformers believed that they rarely, if ever, occurred, and when they did occur, their purpose was only to demonstrate the divinity of Christ as defined by the scriptures.

While Calvin embraced a cessationist doctrine to counter the Catholic Church, Martin Luther believed in a greater leaning on the Holy Spirit that has been misconstrued by modern cessationists. Luther (1483-1546) prayed for the healing of the sick, deliverance of demons, and the prophetic gift, proclaiming, "Often has it happened, and still does; also by calling on the name and prayer, the sick have been healed."[13] Johann Mathesius mentions numerous prophecies given by Luther that were fulfilled.[14]

Yet, when confronted by the Catholic Church to prove his own authority by miracles, Luther argued that miracles were no longer needed to validate the authority of one who stood upon scripture. Luther made his appeal to *sola Scriptura* in front of his accusers. Cessationists construe this to mean he did not believe in the gifts, even though he practiced them. Luther's statement, taken out of context, was used by Benjamin Warfield of Princeton School of Theology in

1918 in his book *Counterfeit Miracles*. There he stated that the Lord had not done a single miracle since the death of the original apostles and those associated with them.[15] As demonstrated throughout church history, however, Warfield was wrong in his assumption that the gifts ended when the last apostle died. He validated his theology by carefully choosing corroborating examples from church history while ignoring others such as Augustine and Luther, who saw miracles, healings, prophecy, and deliverance in their ministries. Thus, he highlighted Calvin with his non-biblical view of miracles.

Despite Calvin's cessationist theological leanings, other early reformers showed a propensity towards the charismata. One such person was John Welch (1568-1622) of Scotland. John considered his day ill spent if he did not pray seven to eight hours a day.[16] On one occasion, it is noted, a minister walking by Welch's place happened to look in the window and saw a strange light surrounding Welch and heard him speak strange words about his spiritual joy.[17] One night, while Welch was a prisoner in the Edinburgh Castle, Lord Ochiltree asked him to preach. When he started to preach, a young man began to mock him and make strange faces at him; Welch told his audience to be quiet and to watch the work of the Lord. The scoffer sank down and died under the table.[18] It is also recorded that Welch prayed for the dead and saw them come back to life after hours of intercession.

John Knox (1514-1572) is credited as the founder of the Presbyterian Church. Knox met Calvin in Geneva in 1554. Unlike Calvin, Knox is known for his intense prayer life and prophetic utterances.[19] Knox battled the same issues with the Catholic Church as Calvin, but influenced by his friend George Wishart, who prophesied,[20] Knox not only didn't deny the gifts, but actually prophesied himself. Knox's gifting put fear into Mary, Queen of Scots; it also helped him transform the nation of Scotland and bring about a revival.

We in the west have been deeply impacted by the Reformation. The Reformation was sorely needed to get us back to the Bible, but its great downside for us is the discrediting of miracles for today.

And this despite the historical evidence of the pouring out of God's power in the first Great Awakening in America in the 18th century.

John Wesley, Jonathan Edwards, and George Whitefield all were highly influential in the first Great Awakening. A brief overview of the ministries of each of these men will show how instrumental they were in releasing God's powerful touch on mankind.

John Wesley viewed the mystical literature as a path to holiness.[21] He recorded in his journal strange outbreaks of the Spirit that occurred during his messages. Some later Methodist historians concluded that these exercises were a manifestation of an initial emotion-driven and "immature" stage of ministry. This is simply not true. The manifestations--fallings, screams, and even holy laughter--continued to break out throughout Wesley's long life and the revivals of other Methodist preachers as the revival continued. Nonetheless, Wesley had his fair share of critics. As De Artega states, "The sophisticated and pharisaical opposition came from the better-educated clergy."[22] Bishop George Lavington (1683-1762) is identified by most historians as the great and influential "opposer" (and Pharisee) of Methodism.[23] Lavington venomously opposed Wesley and the effects of the Spirit upon the Methodist revival participants.

Lavington was offended by the Methodists' outdoor preaching, especially the "exercises" and "enthusiasm" (people falling to the ground, crying, shaking, and other demonstrative events) demonstrated at Methodist services. Lavington called Wesley a Pharisee and attributed the revival manifestations to psychological disturbances and demonic intervention. The revival enthusiasm was a sign to Lavington that John Wesley was a true Pharisee who could not discern the move of the Holy Spirit in the Methodist movement. His widely circulated book, *The Enthusiasm of Methodists and Papists Considered,* published in 1747, attempted to confirm the worst suspicions of the antagonistic Anglican clergy: Methodism was little more than a repetition and concentration of the errors of Catholic mystical extremism.[24] Wesley did not change his apologetic; he continued to present the gospel in a manner that had the charismatic overtones of Acts 2, with bystanders thinking the people where drunk, i.e., drunk people who were falling down and swooning as if under the influence of alcohol.

Jonathan Edwards also saw the manifestations of the Spirit when he spoke. In 1746, Edwards combined a three-part series into one manuscript entitled *Religious Affections* to help explain the effects of the Spirit. It was common that people stirred by his sermons might faint, scream, writhe or thrash about, sing, or otherwise respond physically. Edwards and his colleagues taught that these symptoms might indicate a genuine conviction of sin—or they might be only an emotional response to a manipulative preacher. Edwards claimed that physical manifestations not produced by the working of God did not discredit those that were, in fact, produced by the Spirit.[25]

Edwards wrote, "True religion consists so much in the affections that there can be no true religion without them. He who has no religious affection is in a state of spiritual death, and is wholly destitute of the powerful, quickening, saving influences of the Spirit of God upon his heart. As there is no true religion where there is nothing else but affection, so there is no true religion where there is no religious affection."[26] For Edwards, an unemotional encounter with God could never be God.

John Wesley is known as founder of the Methodist movement, but George Whitefield formed the first Methodist society. In fact, Whitefield pioneered most methods used in the evangelical awakenings of the 1700s: preaching in fields rather than churches, publishing a magazine, and holding conferences. He is best remembered, however, for his part in the first Great Awakening in America, where his preaching had a tremendous impact. He preached to thousands of people; great crowds traveled long distances on horseback to hear him. Benjamin Franklin, Whitefield's friend, once calculated that (in a day before loudspeakers) Whitefield could make his voice heard by 30,000 people![27] The building Franklin built for Whitefield to preach in is located at Philadelphia and later became part of the University of Pennsylvania. Whitefield had many of the same charismatic experiences as did Wesley and Edwards.

As this brief overview shows, throughout church history many of the foundational leaders in the early church (Irenaeus, Augustine), through the Reformation (Luther, Knox), and into the revivals of the 18th century (Wesley, Edwards, Whitefield) saw their ministries marked by experiences in the charismata. The outpouring of God's Spirit is present in all of the major revival moves of both past and present.

Notes

1   Eusebius A. Stephanou, "Charismata in the Early Church Fathers," *Greek Orthodox Theological Review 21 no.2* (Summer 1976), 127.

2   Ralph P. Martin and Peter H. Davids, *Dictionary of the Later New Testament and Its Developments*, (Downers Grove: Intervarsity Press, 2000), electronic ed.

3   Michael William Holmes, *The Apostolic Fathers: Greek Texts and English Translations, Updated ed.* (Grand Rapids: Baker Books, 1999), 263–265.

4   J. A. Draper, *The Apostolic Fathers: The Didache.* (The Expository Times Feb. 2006 vol.117) (5): 177–81. The date of *The Didache* is late first or early second century as argued by J.A. Draper, who disputes that it was an earlier document.

5   Walter A. Elwell and Philip Wesley Comfort, *Tyndale Bible Dictionary, Tyndale Reference Library.* (Wheaton: Tyndale House Publishers, 2001), 1193.

6   Harold R. Holmyard, "The Prophets as Preachers," *Journal of the Evangelical Theological Society Volume 40, 4* (Lynchburg: The Evangelical Theological Society, 1997), 612.

7   "The Pastor of Hermas," F. Crombie, trans., in *The Ante-Nicene Fathers, Volume II: Fathers of the Second Century: Hermas, Tatian, Athenagoras, Theophilus, and Clement of Alexandria (Entire)*, ed., 40.

8   Irenaeus of Lyons, "Irenæus Against Heresies," Alexander Roberts, James Donaldson, and A. Cleveland Coxe, trans., in *The Ante-Nicene Fathers, Volume I: The Apostolic Fathers With Justin Martyr and Irenaeus*, ed. (Buffalo: Christian Literature Company, 1885), 409.

9   Philip Schaff and Henry Wace, "The Ecclesiastical History of Sozomen: Introduction," in *A Select Library of the Nicene and Post-Nicene Fathers of the Christian Church, Second Series, Volume II: Socrates, Sozomenus: Church Histories.* (New York: Christian Literature Company, 1890), 202-03.

10 Augustine, *The City of God*, Marcus Dods, trans., in *A Select Library of the Nicene and Post-Nicene Fathers of the Christian Church, First Series, Volume II:*

St. Augustine's City of God and Christian Doctrine, Philip Schaff, ed. (Buffalo: Christian Literature Company, 1887),8:485.

11 Ruthven, *What's Wrong with Protestant Theology?*, 10.

12 Bromiley, *The International Standard Bible Encyclopedia, Revised, vol. 3*, 378.

13 A.J. Gordon, *The Ministry of Healing.* (Harrisburg: Christian Publications, 1961), 92.

14 Eddie L. Hyatt, *2000 Years of Charismatic History.* (Lake Mary: Charisma House, 2002), 74.

15 Benjamin B. Warfield, *Counterfeit Miracles.* (New York: Charles Scribner's Sons, 1918), 23-24.

16 John Howie, *The Scots Worthies.* (Edinburgh: The Banner of Truth, 1870, reprinted 1995), 120.

17 Howie, *The Scots Worthies*, 124.

18 Howie, *The Scots Worthies*, 130.

19 Howie, *The Scots Worthies*, 57. The Queen Regent was said to be more afraid of Knox' prayers than of an army of 10,000 men. While confined in the castle of St. Andrews, Knox prophesied both the manner of their surrender and their deliverance from the French galleys; when the French army twice discomfited the Lords of the Congregation, he assured them that the Lord would ultimately prosper the work of the Reformation. He is noted as prophesying the beheading of Queen Mary.

20 Howie, *The Scots Worthies*, 23. George Wishart prophesied his death and the manner in which it would occur.

21 Robert G. Tuttle, Jr., *Mysticism in the Wesleyan Tradition.* (Grand Rapids: Francis Asbury Press, 1989), 58-63.

22 William L. De Arteaga, *Forging a Renewed Hebraic and Pauline Christianity.* (Tulsa: Word & Spirit Press, forthcoming), 168.

23 De Arteaga, *Forging*, 169.

24 George Lavington, *The Enthusiasm of Methodists and Papists Considered.* (London: G. and B. Whitaker, Sherwood & Co. 1820), Pt.1, 32. Lavington, in his criticisms of the Methodists, recorded for us what happened in Wesley's meetings. People fell down, laughed, cried, and Wesley experienced Holy Spirit explosions in which the doors and windows of the sanctuary blew out.

25 Guy Chevreau, *Catch the Fire: The Toronto Blessing—An Experience of Renewal and Revival.* (London: Marshall Pickering, 1994) 77.

26 John M. Murrin, et al., *Liberty, Equality, Power: A History of the American People.* (United States: Wadsworth CENGAGE Learning, 2010)

27 "George Whitefield," *Christian History, Issue 38, (Vol. XII, No. 2).* (Carol Stream: Christianity Today, 1993), 3.

Chapter Eight

Why the Gifts are for Today

I was told when I first saw a miracle that this stuff doesn't happen today; that it ended with death of John. That statement so rocked my world that it caused me to question my belief in Christ. I never doubted His reality, just His relevance in my life. What use is a God who once did mighty things but either cannot or will not do them today? But He is still doing them today; the problem is that many churches teach otherwise. In order to demonstrate that spiritual gifts are for today in the church, let's take a short trip through some church history. It's not that the gifts stopped operating in the church today; they haven't. But too many churches and leaders have stopped teaching people how to operate in them. Hopefully this overview will renew your hope that we can still do this today.

Cessationism is the view that the gifts of the Holy Spirit, especially the "sign" gifts—healing, miracles, prophecy, speaking in tongues—ceased with the death of John, the last apostle. Proponents of this view claim that Paul's ministry gives evidence that the gifts were being taken out in the fact Paul could not effect many miracles toward the end of his ministry. They also insist that once the canon of scripture was complete, the gifts went away because they were no longer needed. One reason Paul did not do as many miracles at the end of his ministry was because he was in prison (hence, the "Prison Epistles.") If gifts ended with the last apostle then we should find no historical accounts of miracles flowing through the church. But we do. Paul wrote his letters to the Corinthians somewhere around 55 A.D, while John, the last surviving apostle, died sometime in the mid to late 90s A.D. Are we to seriously consider that the gifts of the Spirit were active and valid for only 45 years? Even using the canon of scripture as the cut-off indicator is problematic. Even though all the writings that make up our New Testament were composed prior to 100 A.D., the final content of the accepted canon was not formalized for another 300 years.

The cessationist view would have made no sense to the early church of 55 A.D. They were actively operating in the gifts and had an eschatology that anticipated the imminent return of Christ in their lifetime. They knew the spiritual gifts validated Jesus Christ as King and Messiah. When Paul said in 1 Corinthians 13:10 that the "partial" (the gifts) would be "done away" when the "perfect" came, by "perfect" did he mean the completion of the biblical canon, or the return of Christ? The early church didn't have a doctrine for the canonization of scripture, but they did for Christ's return.

In Luke 24:49, the risen Christ says to His disciples, "And behold, I am sending for the promise of My Father upon you; but you are to stay in the city until you are clothed with power from on high.". Luke reiterates this instruction from the Lord early in the first chapter of the Book of Acts, the sequel to his Gospel: "And while staying with them he ordered them not to depart from Jerusalem, but to **wait for the promise of the Father**, which, he said, 'you heard from me' (Acts 1:4 ESV, emphasis added).

Why did they need to wait? Didn't they already have the Holy Spirit? If we think linearly, it goes like this: Jesus is crucified on the cross and buried. Three days later he rises from the grave. For the next 40 days He dwells on the earth and appears multiple times to His followers, on one occasion to over 500 people at once. Many saw Him alive and risen from the grave after His death (1 Cor. 15:6).

John 20:21-22 records one significant event that occurred during this 40-day period between Jesus' resurrection and His ascension: [21]"So Jesus said to them again, 'Peace be with you; as the Father has sent Me, I also send you.' [22]And when He had said this, He breathed on them and said to them, 'Receive the Holy Spirit.'" Later, as we have seen, He instructs them to wait in the city until He sends the promise of the Father and they receive power from on high. Then Jesus ascends into heaven and the church waits together as they were commanded, praying and worshiping as they await the coming of the promise.

So, prior to the day of Pentecost, the disciples had already received the Holy Spirit. Why did they need to wait for the promise? Acts 2 describes the momentous events that occurred in Jerusalem on the Day of Pentecost: a mighty rushing wind is heard, tongues of fire descend onto the believers' heads, and the believers start speaking in tongues. All this strange activity draws a curious crowd, and Peter explains to them what is going on: "Being therefore exalted at the right hand of God, and having received from the Father the promise of the Holy Spirit, he has poured out this that you yourselves are seeing and hearing" (Acts 2:33 ESV). A few verses later, he says, "For the promise is for you and for your children and for all who are far off, everyone whom the Lord our God calls to himself" (Acts 2:39 ESV).

Did you catch that? In the context of Acts 2, Jesus is pouring out the Holy Spirit to the people who are there. He then says that this is for you, your children, and to as many as God calls to Himself. So, has God quit calling people to Himself? This promise was a fulfillment of Joel 2, that men servants and maid servants would prophesy. Peter referred to this passage earlier in his address to the crowd: [17]"And in the last days **it shall be**, God declares, that I will pour out my Spirit on all flesh, and **your sons and your daughters shall prophesy**, and your young men shall see visions, and your old men shall dream dreams; [18]even on my male servants and female servants in those days I will pour out my Spirit, and they shall prophesy" (Acts 2:17-18 ESV, emphasis added).

Our new covenant in Christ came with a major upgrade over the old covenant: we are now hardwired to hear His voice. Yet, some today still insist that operating in the gifts of the Spirit doesn't happen anymore. Can anyone show anywhere in the Bible a clear doctrinal pattern that says the gifts have ceased and are no longer in operation? Is there a biblical command anywhere that tells us not to exercise these gifts? Clearly not. On the contrary, Paul encourages us to earnestly desire spiritual gifts; he warns us not to forbid speaking in tongues, or to despise prophetic utterances; and he expresses the desire that we all may prophesy (1 Cor.14:1, 31, 39; 1 Th. 5:20).

Cessationism teaches that all such supernatural manifestations have ended. Benjamin Warfield, a Princeton theologian of the early 20th century and a staunch cessationist, was adamant to protect the concept that after the final revelation of Christ, there could be "no new gospel.[1] Writing in his 1918 book *Counterfeit Miracles*, Warfield claims, "God the Holy Spirit has made it His subsequent work, not to introduce new and unneeded revelations into the world, but to diffuse this one complete revelation through the world and to bring mankind into saving knowledge of it."[2] As a cessationist, Warfield excluded any possibility of any activity of the power of the Holy Spirit in our lives today. He drew support for his views from John Calvin, who wrote that any miracle is a delusion of Satan that draws people away from the true worship of God.[3] Dallas Willard calls Warfield's view "biblical deism."[4]

The message of the kingdom of Jesus is in signs, wonders, and miracles, all of which were carried on by the early church (1 Cor.12:12; Acts 2:22, 43; 6:8; 8:13; Heb. 2:4). The historical evolution of cessationism has roots in Judaism. Cessationism is not a new argument for the ending of the miraculous. The Mishnah and Talmud both had a cessationist polemic that was used against early charismatic Christians.[5] The belief was that with the completion of the Pentateuch, God no longer did miracles. Calvin turned the cessationist polemic against Roman Catholicism and any other authority based upon miracles, and this still affects us today with Reformed theology.[6]

"The Charismatic Spirit manifests the Advance of the Kingdom of God," says Ruthven.[7] Hebrews 2:4 states, "God also testifying with them, both by signs and wonders and by various miracles and by gifts of the Holy Spirit according to His own will." Therefore, the charismata, the gifts, are essential to reveal God's kingdom to mankind. The New Testament teaches that Jesus' ministry was to bring in the kingdom of God via charismatic power.[8]

The clear statements of scripture regarding the charismata are unfriendly to cessationism or the belief that God quit doing miracles. Warfield, in his theological arguments against the charismatic gifts, ignored biblically explicit conditions and commands for the Holy Spirit.[9] The Bible must always dictate our attitude towards people, God, and His gifts. When it comes to loving God and people, the Bible says that we are to love our neighbor as ourselves and love God with all our heart. I think many of us would agree that this is normative biblical value and pursuit. Spiritual gifts come with an attitude that we need to pursue with them zealously. We are to burn with passion in our pursuit of spiritual gifts. First Corinthians14:1 says, "...earnestly desire (*zeloo* -to burn with zeal) spiritual gifts and especially that you may prophesy." So, an unbiblical attitude toward spiritual gifts (the nine listed in 1 Cor. 12 would be in the context of this passage) would be to not chase them with a fervent heart, to say, "Well, they don't really mean anything to me, so why go after them?" We go after them because we are encouraged to do so by the canonized words of Paul. The power of God is all part of His lordship and nature as King Jesus. Jesus as King has established new and better promises for us.

Notes

1   Warfield, *Counterfeit Miracles*, 27. Warfield, a devout cessationist, wrote *Counterfeit Miracles* from a series of six lectures he presented in 1917 at Columbia Theological Seminary. It was his response to the faith healings and revival movements occurring in his time. Warfield believed that the heathen, upon their conversion, were bringing miracle stories into the church (lecture 1-3). William R. Cane, *Miracles Yesterday and Today*, (WRS Journal 14:2, August 2007) 28-34.

2   Warfield, *Counterfeit Miracles*, 26.

3   Pavel Hejzlar, *John Calvin and the Cessation of Miraculous Healing* (Communio Viatorim XLIX Number 1, 2007), 31-77. An abstract of Hejzlar's argument reads: "Calvin's doctrine of cessation of miraculous healing is principally based on two propositions. First, they have fulfilled their function of certifying the gospel when it was new, and second, what really matters is the healing of the soul from sin. Calvin's general Christian-platonic background with hermeneutical principle of analogy and similitude plays in this respect crucial role. In this hermeneutical approach miracles are applied to the present, earthly things to heaven ones, material to the spiritual ones. Calvin shares general platonic conviction about body as a prison of the soul. Physical healing is in fact compared to spiritual one totally unimportant. More reserved attitude toward miracles compared to the older tradition, for example Augustinian, is caused also by catholic-protestant polemic in 16th century. Calvin reads synoptic gospels through the eyes of Gospel of John and miracles function here as signs confirming the proclamation of the true doctrine. Since the Romanist doctrine is far from being sound, no miracle can save it. In addition to this, Calvin insists that even in times when miraculous healing was imparted, it was confined to a narrow group of pre-selected individuals."

4   Willard, *Hearing God*, 142. Biblical deism is the belief that God has given us the Bible and no longer interacts with man with miracles, signs, or wonders, since that would be added revelation.

5   F. E. Greenspahn, *Why Prophecy Ceased*. (JBL 108/ 1, Spring, 1989),37-39.

6   Ruthven, *What's Wrong With Protestant Theology?*, 172.

7   Ruthven, *What's Wrong With Protestant Theology?*, 174.

8   Ruthven, *What's Wrong With Protestant Theology?*, 175.

9   Ruthven, *What's Wrong With Protestant Theology?*, 182. In chapter one of *Counterfeit Miracles*, Warfield argues for the cessation of the charismata.

Chapter Nine

Understanding Christ's Kingdom

*The Kingdom of God must never be reduced to talk, ideas, and prin-
ciples. The kingdom of God is in power.*   – Bill Johnson

For the kingdom of God does not consist in words but in power.
(1 Corinthians 4:20)

There is a correlation between miracles and the gospel of the kingdom that Jesus preached. It is important that we recognize and
understand the flow and power that the Holy Spirit has had on gen-
erations of people. This is why we examined in chapter 7 the historical and biblical theme of the charismata as an apologetic throughout
Bible times into the Reformation and the Evangelical Revivals of
the 18th century. The life and ministry of Jesus emanated a theology
of a triumphant King whose domain has dominion over sickness,
disease, and the demonic.

Christ's victorious kingdom demonstrated His superiority over
other gods and was the primary vehicle that led to the exponential
growth of the early church in Rome.[1]. If we are going to see His
kingdom propagated throughout this earth, we need to be "fully
in"; not lukewarm, but committed to seeing His kingdom prolifer-
ate throughout the earth. A seeker-sensitive or word-of-faith gospel
message diminishes Christianity to little more than getting what we
want in order to be self-actualized or fulfilled. Personal happiness is
the chief goal of such a diluted gospel. The problem with happiness

is that it is fleeting, fragile; it is situational, grounded on external circumstances rather than on eternal principles. Jesus said, "But seek first the kingdom of God and his righteousness, and all these things will be added to you" (Mt. 6:33). I love how the Lord sets our priorities for us!

If you had asked me many years ago, "What is the kingdom of God and what does it mean to be a kingdom person?" I probably would have answered, "Well, I guess it's where we all go as Christians when we die; it's heaven." A few years ago, God showed me how wrong I was. But I believe many Christians still think that way. Many believers really don't know exactly what the kingdom of God is. They may not think of it as much more than as a good talking point for starting a spiritual conversation with someone. God began to change the way that I viewed His kingdom, and He also began to give me a passion for His kingdom and for growing it in the here and now.

A kingdom has four basic elements:

1)   a king, supreme ruler, or governing agent;
2)   territory, with its specific location and definite boundary lines
3)   subjects or citizens within that territorial jurisdiction
4)   laws and a form of government through which the will of the ruler is exercised.

If we ignore any one of these essential elements—if we ignore the message that Jesus Christ brought from the Father—we will have a distorted faith, one that will not bring salvation.

Ken Hemphill says, "In the kingdom of God, I have found something far superior to personal fulfillment. I have found the heart of God. I have found my reason for being here."[2] I think it's the same for me. Since I've stepped out in obedience to God's call (which required a lot of change inside me in both my thoughts and my actions, as well as a lot of moving around) I have seen God at work not only in my life, but also in the world around me. As a result, I am completely convinced that *the kingdom's sheer immensity removes all limits on what God can do through us.*

Why is the kingdom of God so important? For one thing, the kingdom is the primary theme of the New Testament, being mentioned 126 times in the Gospels and 34 times in the rest of the NT. The first recorded sermon in the New Testament is John the Baptist's one-line appeal, "Repent, for the kingdom of heaven has come near" (Mt. 3:2 NIV).

In a kingdom, there is a king. A kingdom literally means, "The king's domain." This is an obscure concept for us since we live in a republic that expresses itself in a democratic mindset. We have rights guaranteed to us by the Constitution. We are not subjects but citizens. As citizens, we believe that we are all equal. In a kingdom, the king is the supreme being. So when we call Jesus Lord, we are saying, "You are my master." The kingdom creates a realm, and the kingdom creates a people, but the kingdom of God is not synonymous either with its realm or its people.

Jesus began His ministry with the same message: *"From that time on Jesus began to preach, 'Repent, for the kingdom of heaven has come near'"* (Mt. 4:17 NIV). And His ministry ended the same way: *"After his suffering, he presented himself to them and gave many convincing proofs that he was alive. He appeared over a period of forty days and spoke about the kingdom of God"* (Acts 1:3 NIV). With Jesus, there is a correlation between the kingdom and people getting healed in Matthew 4. Jesus, in talking about His kingdom, is saying, "In my kingdom, I have defeated death and disease." He is a triumphant King, a victorious King, a King who has called us to be in His kingdom. Unlike an earthly kingdom, in His kingdom, we are sons and daughters of the King.

The kingdom was the central theme of the public ministry of the Lord Jesus. Everywhere He went, Jesus preached the gospel of His kingdom in the context of people being healed and set free from all kinds of afflictions and demonic oppression: "And he went throughout all Galilee, teaching in their synagogues and **proclaiming the**

**gospel of the kingdom and healing every disease and every afflic-
tion among the people**" (Mt. 4:33 ESV, emphasis added).

*⁴⁰Now when the sun was setting, all those who had any who were sick with
various diseases brought them to him, and he laid his hands on every one of
them and healed them. ⁴¹And demons also came out of many, crying, "You
are the Son of God!" But he rebuked them and would not allow them to
speak, because they knew that he was the Christ. ⁴²And when it was day,
he departed and went into a desolate place. And the people sought him and
came to him, and would have kept him from leaving them, ⁴³but he said
to them, "I must preach the good news of the kingdom of God to the other
towns as well; for I was sent for this purpose"* (Luke 4:40–43 ESV).

And it's not just the New Testament. The kingdom of God is also
the central teaching of the Old Testament:

*On that day Yahweh will become king over all the earth—Yahweh alone,
and His name alone* (Zechariah 14:9 HCSB).

*Saviors will ascend Mount Zion to rule over the hill country of Esau, but
the kingdom will be the LORD's* (Obadiah 1:21 HCSB).

*He was given authority to rule, and glory, and a kingdom; so that those of
every people, nation, and language should serve Him. His dominion is an
everlasting dominion that will not pass away, and His kingdom is one that
will not be destroyed* (Daniel 7:14 HCSB).

Many other Old Testament passages convey the same message.
As God established Israel as a nation and as He called them back to
a relationship with Him, His concern was His kingdom.

In a way that we cannot completely understand, we are sons and
daughters of God in His kingdom: "and I will be a father to you, and
you shall be sons and daughters to me, says the Lord Almighty" (2
Cor. 6:18 ESV). *If we are subjects in the kingdom of God, then God is the
ruler of our lives.* He is our King and His kingdom is in the world now
because we are in the world representing Him. If we are to understand the kingdom of God, we must know what the kingdom of God

is: the realm over which He has dominion. Because we are His sons and daughters, the kingdom should play a significantly greater part in our lives than we normally think. We have been adopted by the King, and that is of inestimable value. In ancient Roman culture, an adopted son or daughter experienced four major changes: a change of family, a change of name, a change of home, and a change of responsibilities.[3] Under Roman law, an adopted person ceased entirely to be a member of his or her own former family and came under the power and authority of a new head of family, the paterfamilias.

In Ancient Roman times, the adopting of boys among upper class families was a fairly common practice. Unlike adoptions today, adoptions in ancient Rome almost always were for political reasons. Julius Caesar, for example, who had no legitimate male heir, chose Octavian as his adopted son. Upon Caesar's death, Octavian, as heir, received two-thirds of Caesar's estate. More importantly, as Caesar's adopted son, Octavian managed to garner the support of 3000 veteran soldiers who had been loyal to his adopted father, as well as win two of Mark Antony's legions. Had Caesar not adopted Octavian as his heir, Octavian would never have gained the political and military support he needed to become the first Emperor of Rome. Likewise, as adopted sons and daughters of God, we have been given a new name, new authority, and a new King.

Understanding the kingdom of God can be a challenge because it encompasses so many things. Here are just a few:

- In a mysterious way, the kingdom has come and yet is still to come; it is here now but yet not here (fully). The kingdom is revealed today in the life of the church and the lives of individual believers, but will be perfectly revealed, expressed, and experienced at the second coming of Christ when He establishes His kingdom rule on the earth.
- The kingdom is revealed in obedience to the will of God by individual believers and by the corporate body of the church.
- The kingdom is a reality whenever and wherever when obedience to God's Word and will is a reality.

- The kingdom is the opposite of selfishness, arrogance, and human manipulation.
- The kingdom is seen whenever God's revelation through His Word is obeyed and His presence through the Holy Spirit is realized.

As wonderful as all of this sounds (and it is wonderful), it is important to understand that there is a cost to following Jesus. It is more than just saying a little prayer; prayer is the access gate for entering God's kingdom. And while prayer certainly should continue, kingdom living involves the surrender of your very life and will. If the King is Lord of your life, you will love the things the King loves and hate the things the King hates. That is what subjects do; they fulfill the desires of the King as their first priority primary, giving second-place to their own desires. As loving sons and daughters, we want to please our Father, who is the King. As His sons and daughters, we are to be instruments God can use to extend His kingdom everywhere and all the time.

Simply stated, then, a kingdom enterprise is where the power of God is evident, the presence of God is experienced, and the purposes of God are realized. *But here's the best thing about all of this: The kingdom of God is God's gift to us and it comes in power.* As our Father does, so also can we do; it's in our spiritual DNA once we are born again. When we are born again (John 3:3), we leave the kingdom of darkness and come into God's kingdom of light, where He delegates authority to us as His ambassadors to represent Him and His kingdom in the world.

And he called to him his twelve disciples and gave them authority over unclean spirits, to cast them out, and to heal every disease and every affliction (Matthew 10:1 ESV).

7 "And proclaim as you go, saying, 'The kingdom of heaven is at hand.' 8 Heal the sick, raise the dead, cleanse lepers, cast out demons. You received without paying; give without pay" (Matthew 10:7–8 ESV).

84

"But if it is by the finger of God that I cast out demons, then the kingdom of God has come upon you" (Luke 11:20 ESV).

The kingdom of God is reserved for those who hear, commit, and prepare. It is His gift to us. We cannot—must not—be passive about the King's rule in our lives. The greatness of His gift calls for a life of the most strenuous vigilance, labor, perseverance—and radical obedience. The King gave His ultimate gift to us; in return, we must give our ultimate allegiance to the King and His kingdom. Are you prepared to obey God's command to proclaim His kingdom to the world? Are you "all-in," committed totally to the King?

If you are, it will cost you. (But the rewards are out of this world!)

The kingdom of heaven is like treasure, buried in a field, that a man found and reburied. Then in his joy he goes and sells everything he has and buys that field (Matthew 13:44 (HCSB).

Jesus tells a parable likening the kingdom of heaven to treasure buried in a field, where a man stumbles upon it unexpectedly. Realizing the value of what he has found, he quickly reburies it. Then he hurries off in joyous excitement, sells everything he owns, and buys the field. What a wise investment he made! He was willing to sell everything he had in order to get a treasure worth more than anything else—and which he could never lose.

Did you view the kingdom of God that way when you entered it? When you received Jesus into your heart and made Him Lord of your life, did you give up everything to serve Him? We cannot have salvation without a cost—or without the cross. There is no costless or cross-less salvation. In *The Cost of Discipleship*, German theologian and pastor Dietrich Bonhoeffer described the cost of following Jesus succinctly and memorably: "When Christ calls a man, he bids him come and die." Elaborating on this idea, he continues:

Costly grace is the gospel which must be *sought* again and again and again, the gift which must be *asked* for, the door at which a man must *knock*.

Such grace is *costly* because it calls us to follow, and it is *grace* because it calls us to follow *Jesus Christ*. It is costly because it costs a man his life, and it is grace because it gives a man the only true life. It is costly because it condemns sin, and grace because it justifies the sinner. Above all, it is *costly* because it cost God the life of his Son: "ye were bought at a price," and what has cost God much cannot be cheap for us. Above all, it is *grace* because God did not reckon his Son too dear a price to pay for our life, but delivered him up for us. Costly grace is the Incarnation of God."[4]

Here is a little test to see if Jesus is truly your King. Ask yourself, "What is most important to me? What do I spend most of my money and time on?" Then examine your answer to see where the kingdom of God fits into it. Is Jesus truly the Lord of your life? Are you really a kingdom person?

In Jesus' parable of the lost treasure, the man who found the hidden treasure had to decide whether or not to purchase it because to do so would cost him everything. He had to take a personal inventory and ask, "Is this treasure I just found more valuable than the treasures that I have now in my possession?" Deciding that it was, he sold everything he had in order to buy the field and claim the treasure. Are you ready to pay the cost of being a kingdom person? If you are, God will bless you beyond measure and give you more than you ever dreamed.

God's kingdom is the only kingdom that will last forever. You can't stop it from growing and you can't make it grow. It is God's kingdom, and it *will* grow because He will make it grow. Everything that God has done—all the things that you learned in the Bible, all the blessings that God has bestowed on his people, everything that God has blessed you with—is intended to have a global and eternal impact. But it means that you have to change the way you think about what is truly important. A person once told me that he was not willing to give up his lifestyle to pursue God's call on his life. This is what Jesus means when he says that we cannot serve God and mammon: "No one can serve two masters, for either he will hate the one and love the other, or he will be devoted to the one and despise the other. You cannot serve God and money" (Matthew 6:24 ESV). To put it another way: If Jesus is King, then who sits on the throne of your life?

If we are going to touch a culture, we must be sold out to God's kingdom. Otherwise, we have never left the old kingdom. The kingdoms of this earth value wealth; the kingdom of heaven says to sell all. The kingdoms of earth value power; the kingdom of heaven values servants:

> ^{24}*A dispute also arose among them, as to which of them was to be regarded as the greatest.* ^{25}*And he said to them, "The kings of the Gentiles exercise lordship over them, and those in authority over them are called benefactors.* ^{26}*But not so with you. Rather, let the greatest among you become as the youngest, and the leader as one who serves.* ^{27}*For who is the greater, one who reclines at table or one who serves? Is it not the one who reclines at table? But I am among you as the one who serves.*
>
> ^{28}*"You are those who have stayed with me in my trials,* ^{29}*and I assign to you, as my Father assigned to me, a kingdom,* ^{30}*that you may eat and drink at my table in my kingdom and sit on thrones judging the twelve tribes of Israel"* (Luke 22:24–30 ESV).

If we are going to change the world, we cannot allow the world to change us. Jesus wants us to be transformed, to morph into His kingdom person and not be conformed to the world. There are no Christian celebrities in the kingdom of God; the King has adopted each one of us to serve Him. Today, we can all hear His voice (John 10:27); we all have the ability to effect miracles. This is part of the New Testament, the new and better covenant promised to us.

Notes

1   Ramsay McMullen, *Christianizing The Roman Empire A.D. 100-400.* (New Haven: Yale University Press:1984), 22, 101. The essence of McMullen's book is that Christianity spread rapidly not because of Constantine's rule but because of the signs and wonders following the Christians.

2   Ken Hemphill, *EKG: The Heartbeat of God.* (Nashville: Broadman & Holman Publishers, 2004), 1.

3   W. M. Ramsay, *A Historical Commentary on St. Paul's Epistle to the Galatians.* (Grand Rapids: Baker Book House, 1979 reprint of Hodder and Stoughton 1900 original), p. 353.

4   Dietrich Bonhoeffer, *The Cost of Discipleship.* (New York: Collier Books, Macmillan Publishing Company, 1959), 47-48, emphasis in the original.

Chapter Ten

Who is This Holy Spirit?

The Spirit-filled life is not a special, deluxe edition of Christianity. It is part and parcel of the total plan of God for His people
— A. W. Tozer

The Holy Spirit is a promise from God to us (see Lk. 24:49; Acts 2:39). He is part of the New Testament "upgrade" to us and will never leave us or forsake us; He is with us always. Jesus described the Spirit's purpose in our lives: "However, when He, the Spirit of truth, has come, He will guide you into all truth; for He will not speak on His own *authority*, but whatever He hears He will speak; and He will tell you things to come" (Jn. 16:13 NKJV).

Many misconceptions exist regarding the identity of the Holy Spirit. Some people view the Holy Spirit as a mystical force; others, as an impersonal power that God makes available to followers of Christ. What does the Bible say about the identity of the Holy Spirit? Simply put, the Bible declares that the Holy Spirit is God. Again, *the Holy Spirit is* **God**. He is not an "it." He is not a "divine influence." He is not a fleecy white cloud, a ghost, or a theoretical concept. He is a Person, and as such, possesses a will, an intellect and emotions. The Holy Spirit is God, and thereby is endued with all the attributes of deity. He is the third person of the Trinity, co-equal with God the Father and God the Son. There is only one God, but He manifests Himself in three Persons, whom we call the Trinity.

The Holy Spirit is one of the three Persons of the Godhead: Father, Son, and Holy Spirit. This is a difficult concept for many people to grasp. The Bible unequivocally declares that there is only one true and living God, yet it also reveals Him as three distinct personages; three Persons, yet one essence. One way to partially visualize this concept is to examine the nature of water (H_2O). Water is a single compound that can exist in three states: liquid, ice, and vapor. An egg is another picture: white, yolk, and shell, but still one egg. Another example is a man who is a husband, a father, and a son, yet only one man. At best, these are imperfect analogies that can only suggest a little of what the triune God is like. They in no way convey a complete picture of our God, but they are illustrative of the reality that His three "Persons" in no way invalidate His oneness.

The Holy Spirit is much more than an ethereal life force. Some people have the idea that the Holy Spirit is like "The Force" in *Star Wars*: "The Jedi's strength flows from the Force," says Yoda to young Luke Skywalker. The Holy Spirit, however, is not some vague, nebulous, impersonal and unthinking life force. No, the Holy Spirit is a full "Person" equal in every way to God the Father and God the Son. The Bible tells us that all the characteristics of God apparent in the Father and the Son are equally apparent in the Holy Spirit. Let's let the Bible speak to us clearly and distinctly as to who the Holy Spirit is.

The Holy Spirit possesses the attributes of God. As I mentioned before, the Father, the Son, and the Holy Spirit together comprise a unified Godhead known in Christianity as the Trinity. A common misconception among non-Christians is that Christians believe in three different gods. This is not correct. While each Person of the Trinity is distinct in function, each share equally the same divine essence and reflect the same divine attributes of the one true and living God. Regarding the Holy Spirit, the Bible reveals that:

- *the Holy Spirit is eternal*: "how much more will the blood of Christ, who through the eternal Spirit offered Himself without blemish to God, cleanse your conscience from dead works to serve the living God?" (Heb. 9:14)

- *the Holy Spirit is all-knowing (omniscient)*: "For who among men knows the *thoughts* of a man except the spirit of the man which is in him? Even so the *thoughts* of God no one knows except the Spirit of God" (1 Cor. 2:11).
- *the Holy Spirit is everywhere (omnipresent)*: 7"Where can I go from Your Spirit? Or where can I flee from Your presence? 8If I ascend to heaven, You are there; If I make my bed in Sheol, behold, You are there" (Ps. 139:7-8).

The Holy Spirit possesses the characteristics of personality:

- *the Holy Spirit has a mind*: "And he who searches our hearts knows the mind of the Spirit, because the Spirit intercedes for the saints in accordance with God's will."(Romans 8:27 NIV). "For who among men knows the *thoughts* of a man except the spirit of the man which is in him? Even so the *thoughts* of God no one knows except the Spirit of God" (1 Cor. 2:11).
- *the Holy Spirit has a will*: "But one and the same Spirit works all these things, distributing to each one individually just as He wills" (1 Cor. 12:11).
- *the Holy Spirit has emotions*: "Now I urge you, brethren, by our Lord Jesus Christ and by the love of the Spirit, to strive together with me in your prayers to God for me" (Rom. 15:30). For example, *the Holy Spirit can experience grief*: "And do not grieve the Holy Spirit of God, with whom you were sealed for the day of redemption" (Eph. 4:30 NIV). "Yet they rebelled and grieved his Holy Spirit. So he turned and became their enemy and he himself fought against them" (Is. 63:10 NIV). But also, *the Holy Spirit can experience and give joy*: "At that time Jesus, full of joy through the Holy Spirit, said, 'I praise you, Father, Lord of heaven and earth, because you have hidden these things from the wise and learned, and revealed them to little children. Yes, Father, for this was your good pleasure'" (Lk. 10:21 NIV). "You became imitators of us and of the Lord; in spite of severe

suffering, you welcomed the message with the joy given by the Holy Spirit" (1 Th. 1:6 NIV).

Like any other person, the Holy Spirit can be and often is mistreated by sinful human beings:

- *the Holy Spirit can be lied to*: "Then Peter said, 'Ananias, how is it that Satan has so filled your heart that you have lied to the Holy Spirit and have kept for yourself some of the money you received for the land?'" (Acts 5:3 NIV)
- *the Holy Spirit can be resisted*: "You stiff-necked people, with uncircumcised hearts and ears! You are just like your fathers: You always resist the Holy Spirit!" (Acts 7:51 NIV)
- *the Holy Spirit can be blasphemed*: ³¹"And so I tell you, every sin and blasphemy will be forgiven men, but the blasphemy against the Spirit will not be forgiven. ³²Anyone who speaks a word against the Son of Man will be forgiven, but anyone who speaks against the Holy Spirit will not be forgiven, either in this age or in the age to come" (Mt. 12:31-32 NIV).
- *the Holy Spirit can be quenched*: "Quench not the Spirit" (1 Th. 5:19 KJV).

Although the Holy Spirit has all the characteristics of God, He has specific roles and functions in our lives:

- *the Holy Spirit lives inside us*: "Do you not know that you are the temple of God and *that* the Spirit of God dwells in you?" (1 Cor. 3:16 NKJV)
- *the Holy Spirit gives us our power*: "But you shall receive power, when the Holy Spirit has come upon you" (Acts 1:8a NKJV).
- *the Holy Spirit gives us our direction*: "For as many as are led by the Spirit of God, these are sons of God" (Rom. 8:14 NKJV).
- *the Holy Spirit is there for us in times of weakness and prayer*: "In the same way the Spirit also helps our weakness; for we do not know how to pray as we should, but the Spirit Himself intercedes for *us* with groaning's too deep for words" (Rom. 8:26).

- *the Holy Spirit teaches us*: "But the Counselor, the Holy Spirit, whom the Father will send in my name, will teach you all things and will remind you of everything I have said to you" (Jn. 14:26 NIV).

- *the Holy Spirit testifies of Christ*: "When the Counselor comes, whom I will send to you from the Father, the Spirit of truth who goes out from the Father, he will testify about me" (Jn. 15:26 NIV).

- *the Holy Spirit convicts us (and the world)*: "When he comes, he will convict the world of guilt in regard to sin and righteousness and judgment" (Jn. 16:8 NIV). An alternate translation says, "When he comes, he will expose the guilt of the world."

- *the Holy Spirit leads us*: "because those who are led by the Spirit of God are sons of God" (Rom. 8:14 NIV).

- *the Holy Spirit reveals truth to us*: "But when he, the Spirit of truth, comes, he will guide you into all truth. He will not speak on his own; he will speak only what he hears, and he will tell you what is yet to come" (Jn. 16:13 NIV).

- *the Holy Spirit strengthens and encourages us*: "Then the church throughout Judea, Galilee and Samaria enjoyed a time of peace. It was strengthened; and encouraged by the Holy Spirit, it grew in numbers, living in the fear of the Lord" (Acts 9:31 NIV).

- *the Holy Spirit comforts us*: "And I will pray the Father, and he shall give you another Comforter, that he may abide with you forever;" (John 14:16 KJV)

- *the Holy Spirit helps us in our weakness*: "In the same way, the Spirit helps us in our weakness. We do not know what we ought to pray for, but the Spirit himself intercedes for us with groans that words cannot express" (Rom. 8:26).

- *the Holy Spirit intercedes for us*: "Likewise the Spirit helps us in our weakness. For we do not know what to pray for as we ought, but the Spirit himself intercedes for us with groanings too deep for words. (Rom. 8:26 ESV).

- *the Holy Spirit searches the deep things of God*: [10]"The Spirit searches all things, even the deep things of God. [11]For who among men knows the thoughts of a man except the man's spirit within him?

In the same way no one knows the thoughts of God except the Spirit of God" (1 Cor. 2:10b-11 NIV).

- *the Holy Spirit sanctifies us*: "to be a minister of Christ Jesus to the Gentiles with the priestly duty of proclaiming the gospel of God, so that the Gentiles might become an offering acceptable to God, sanctified by the Holy Spirit" (Rom. 15:16 NIV).
- *the Holy Spirit bears witness or testifies to our salvation*: "The Spirit himself testifies with our spirit that we are God's children" (Rom. 8:16 NIV).
- *the Holy Spirit forbids*: 6"Paul and his companions traveled throughout the region of Phrygia and Galatia, having been kept by the Holy Spirit from preaching the word in the province of Asia. 7When they came to the border of Mysia, they tried to enter Bithynia, but the Spirit of Jesus would not allow them to" (Acts 16:6-7).

It is key to note that as a person, the Holy Spirit is real. He is ever present, and He will make known to you things that you could not know in the natural (1 Cor. 14:25) that will lead people to Jesus.

This is good news for us because sometimes there is a sense that the people in the Bible were superhuman or extraordinary, but the Bible teaches us something completely different. We are bought with a price; we are God's, and He longs for relationship with us. Any healthy relationship is characterized by regular and effective communication between the parties. As we have seen, Jesus promised that the Holy Spirit would tell us of things to come (Jn. 16:13). As Christians, then, we should be listening closely to the Spirit's voice.

The Holy Spirit came to glorify Christ and to lead believers into all truth. He came to comfort and to help us. He came to enable us to know Christ through a new birth and to give us the power to live and share the abundant life that Jesus promised to all who trust and obey Him. The Holy Spirit was sent by God to empower us to be witnesses for Jesus. As witnesses or disciples, we manifest the kingdom of God by demonstrating His power to others (Mt. 10:7-8).

Acts 2:22 tells us that Jesus' credibility, in his claim to being Messiah was attested to, or proven, by signs, wonders, and miracles. John 14:12 declares that those who believe in Christ (Christians, or Christ-followers) will do greater works than He because He went to the Father. Therefore, if Jesus needed signs, wonders, and miracles to attest to His divinity (Acts 2:22), shouldn't we be attesting to Jesus by the same methods? Jesus' promise to us (Lk. 24:49) is the outpouring of His Spirit upon his followers (Acts 2:33, 39).

The Holy Spirit empowers us to be a witness in power (Acts 1:8). It is His power that brought the woman at the well (Jn. 4) to acknowledge that Jesus was the Messiah. It was the healing of the blind man (Jn. 9:37-38) that led him to the revelation that Jesus was the Messiah. Paul said that the Gentiles came to know Jesus by signs and wonders by the power of the Holy Spirit (Rom. 15:18-19).

The Holy Spirit inspired holy men of old to write the scriptures. As you read the Bible, He reveals its truth to you. I have experienced many times reading passages of scripture that I have read many times before, when suddenly, at the exact moment I need a particular truth, a certain familiar passage comes alive to me as never before. Why? The Holy Spirit makes the Word of God relevant and meaningful when I need it. The Bible is a living book inspired by the Spirit.

I cannot live a holy life apart from the help of the Holy Spirit. He gives us fruit and it is good. As Galatians 5:22-23a says, [22]"the fruit of the Spirit is love, joy, peace, patience, kindness, goodness, faithfulness, [23]gentleness and self-control" (NIV).

A minister friend once said to me, "I don't like all of this talk about the Holy Spirit; I am not really into Him. I want to talk about Jesus Christ."

"So, you're not into God?" I asked.

"No, I am into God," he replied, "just not the Holy Spirit."

The Holy Spirit *is* God, and you cannot be into God if you are not into the Holy Spirit. If you are into God, then you need to be into the Father, the Son, *and* the Holy Spirit. I reminded him that the reason the Holy Spirit came was to exalt and glorify Christ. It has never made sense to me to hear people say, "We are not into the Holy Spirit," If the Holy Spirit is God, then logically that statement would mean that they are not into God, or they only want to serve two Persons of the Trinity instead of all three. That is not even possible. It is impossible even to know Christ apart from the regenerating ministry of the Spirit. It was Jesus Himself who said, "Unless one is born of water and the Spirit, he cannot enter the kingdom of God" (Jn. 3:5 ESV). It is impossible for you to become a Christian, to understand the Bible and other spiritual truths such as prayer, to live a holy life, to witness, or do anything else for the Lord Jesus apart from the person of the Holy Spirit. So, if the Holy Spirit is a person, how does He communicate with us?

Chapter Eleven

How to Hear the Person of the Holy Spirit

An important step in getting to know God is to realize how available he is to us. In learning to hear God, it helps us to take on faith the fact that we are already in his presence. If we must make ourselves worthy of his presence first, we will never get there.

– Craig S. Keener[1]

How can anyone experience a personal relationship, whether with God or with a fellow human being, without engaging in individualized communication? Hearing involves both listening and understanding.[2] I would like to share my story of how I first began to hear the Holy Spirit and then give you some practical exercises that you can implement in your own life to help you learn to discern the Spirit's voice for yourself.

I was 22 years old and a student at USC when I had my first encounter with hearing the voice of God. I shared a room with two football players. I spent hours every day reading the Bible with a yellow legal pad close at hand for taking notes. At that time, I perceived prayer as more of a monologue than a dialogue. The Jewish people in the Old Testament, once they had experienced God in a particular way, gave Him a new name that described an attribute of His by which they had come to know Him in a new way. When they saw Him heal, they named Him Jehovah Rapha, the God who heals (Ex. 15:26). They also knew Him as Jehovah Shalom, the God of peace (Jer.9:6). But my God was Jehovah Genie, the God who gives me what I want whenever I pray. I didn't have a paradigm for a transcendent God who wanted to interact with me.

As I progressed in listening to Him, I started asking Him questions and then wrote down what I felt He had said to me. There was some tension in doing this because I thought to myself, "Is this me, or is it really God?" At first, I asked the Lord what He thought of me and why He created me. "I love you Nick," I heard Him say, "and I created you to be with me." I remember crying when I heard this because I felt unlovable and struggled with acceptance from others. How could it be that God loved me? I could understand Him loving someone else, but I had a hard time grasping His love for me personally. As time went on, I continued to ask Him questions and recorded what I felt were His answers.

One day while in prayer, I felt the Lord talk to me about a guy who was in our campus group. JP was a pre-med student at USC and had a very arrogant demeanor towards us. Maybe it was because he was pre-med and we were jocks that he felt superior to us. I had a hard time with him; he was like spiritual sandpaper to me, always rubbing me the wrong way. That day in prayer I felt the Lord say, "Nick, JP has pride in his life, and unless he repents, I am going to take his ministry from him." In the natural, I thought, "This is a great word; God is going to do something about this guy!" but I wasn't sure if this was me or God, so I did nothing about it.

Several days passed and the Lord reminded me during prayer of what I was supposed to do, but again, I did nothing. One day there was a knock on my door and it was JP. He came into my room with a demonstrative demeanor and reprimanded me. "I have a word from God for you," he said. "God is telling me that you are getting words for people and you are not telling them His word." When I heard this, I started to laugh. He became indignant and said, "I see nothing funny in this."

"You will in a minute," I replied.

Brother Lawrence said, "There is not in the world a kind of life more sweet and delightful than that of a continual conversation with God."[3] Normal biblical Christianity is hearing God's voice because God has given His sheep the ability to hear His voice. God is no respecter of persons (Acts 10:34). Jesus said we shall know the truth, and the truth shall make us free (Jn. 8:32). Truth is more than having correct doctrine. Truth is a Person; if you have that Person, you have the truth. One of the outrageous benefits of being a Jesus follower is that He longs for relationship with us. Any healthy relationship includes regular communication between the two parties.

Jesus said, "My sheep hear my voice" (Jn. 10:27). What is frustrating about this is that He doesn't tell us how. Do we have to use an argument from silence as to how His sheep hear His voice, or does the Bible give us some clues?

Here are a few examples of God speaking to man:

- *"God spake unto Noah, saying"* (Genesis 8:15 KJV).
- *"The LORD had said unto Abram ... "* (Genesis 12:1 KJV).
- *"The LORD said unto Moses ... "* (Exodus 24:12 KJV).
- *"Then came the word of the LORD to Isaiah ... "* (Isaiah 38:4 KJV).

What did this look like? Did some special courier bring it to them: "Word of the Lord for Isaiah"? Some assume that God speaks only in an audible voice. Without a doubt, He does speak to us through the Bible.

Elijah's experience will help us understand this a little bit:

[11]*And he [God] said, Go forth, and stand upon the mount before the LORD. And, behold, the LORD passed by, and a great and strong wind rent the mountains, and brake in pieces the rocks before the LORD; but the LORD was not in the wind: and after the wind an earthquake; but the LORD was not in the earthquake:* [12]*And after the earthquake a fire; but the LORD was not in the fire: and after the fire a **still small voice**. And it*

was so, when Elijah heard it, that he … went out, and stood in the entering in of the cave. And, behold, there came a voice unto him, and said, What doest thou here, Elijah? (1 Kings 19:11–13 KJV, emphasis added).

A "still small voice" (KJV); a "gentle whisper" (NIV); "sheer silence" (NRSV). Notice that these words do not describe the loud and really audible voice of the Lord. According to the *Abridged Brown-Driver-Briggs Lexicon*, this word means a sound or a voice, especially a human voice, spoken and recognized.[4] This "still small voice" was recognizable to Elijah. We can assume, then, that one of the ways God speaks to us is in a voice that sounds like a whisper; it can sound a lot like our own voice. In his book, *Is That Really You, God?*, Lauren Cunningham, the founder of Youth With A Mission, talks about his journey in hearing this still small voice.[5] Dallas Willard says this about the still small voice:

> Unfortunately, this gentle low-key word may easily be overlooked or disregarded, and it has even been discounted or despised by some who think that only the more explosive communications can be authentic. For those who follow this view, a life of hearing God must become a life filled with constant fireworks from heaven…
>
> God usually addresses individually those who walk with him in a mature, personal relationship using this inner voice, showing forth the reality of the kingdom of God as they go…
>
> But a major point of this book is that the still, small voice—or the interior or inner voice, as it is also called—is the preferred and most valuable form of individual communication for God's purposes.[6]

Some Christians are skeptical that we can hear God's voice today. Many cessationists, when they say God can't speak today in an individual's life, seem to have created a new "Trinity"; they seem to believe in "The Father, The Son, and the Holy Scriptures." To them, the only way God speaks today is through the Bible.[7] Normal New Testament Christianity is hearing God's voice, because God has given His sheep the ability to hear His voice. This is part of the upgrade we get in the new covenant in Christ, but, for many, it is too good to be true.

As J.P. Moreland, theologian and author of *The Kingdom Triangle*, observes:

> The western church has lagged behind experiencing the power of the Kingdom of God compared to other parts of the world, primarily because we have embraced and accepted a worldview called Naturalism. We tend to believe that the natural world really is all there is, that God heals only through medicine, that spirits are really multiple personality problems and things like that. And people in other parts of the world actually have more of a Biblical worldview when they come to Jesus Christ because they already know that demons are real, they know there's a spiritual world. They automatically believe God for healing because they've seen healing before.[8]

We have talked about hearing God and how that can impact our culture. In the nine gifts listed in 1 Corinthians12, four of them are called revelatory gifts, meaning that they require one to hear God's voice: word of wisdom, word of knowledge, discerning of spirits, and prophecy:

> [8]*For to one is given through the Spirit the utterance of wisdom, and to another the utterance of knowledge according to the same Spirit,* [9]*to another faith by the same Spirit, to another gifts of healing by the one Spirit,* [10]*to another the working of miracles, to another prophecy, to another the ability to distinguish between spirits, to another various kinds of tongues, to another the interpretation of tongues* (1 Corinthians 12:8–10 ESV).

Word of Wisdom is the insight, direction or specific counsel for a situation that is beyond our natural mind to know. It is receiving direction from God on how to do something that you do not know how to do.

1. Noah was told how to build the…Ark.
2. Moses was told how to build the Ark of the Covenant.
3. Joseph was told how to lay up provision to offset the seven years of famine.[9]

I have a friend in Southern California who is an aerospace engineer and owns 13 different patents. One is used as an industry standard on the technology used on the F22 and F35 fighter jets today. I asked him how he did it. He said that one time he was working on the space station on some fiber optic cables and they could not operate correctly. He was using the Monte Carlo method, a series of computational algorithms that obtain numerical results through repeated random sampling. The system was having problems and it would cost an additional 10 million dollars to make sure it worked correctly. My friend said he woke up one morning and the Lord spoke to him and gave him the mathematical solutions as a diagram in his head. He said he had the answer in a moment, but since he is an engineer, it took him another six months to verify that the numbers were correct, and they were.

This differs from a word of knowledge that gives specific information about a person or an event. For example, I was speaking once at a church in Salem, VA. While praying for a young man, I saw in my mind a red brick house with white pillars and the number 2439 in black letters. I asked whether this made any sense to him because it certainly did not to me. He said, "I live in a red brick house that has white pillars, and the address is 2439." I did not possess that information about him, but the Lord did. By the way, this was this man's first time to church and he ended up receiving Jesus as his Lord and Savior.

Discerning of spirits is a supernatural manifestation given by the Holy Spirit that reveals whether a miracle or some other operation or spiritual manifestation is of God or not. Acts 16:16-18 says that the Holy Spirit revealed to Paul that the spirit of the slave girl was demonic and not from God.

Prophecy is a gift that builds, strengthens, and comforts people with the reality of God speaking through man (1 Cor.14:3, 25). As born-again, redeemed children of the Lord, I believe we all have the ability to hear His voice, but I do not believe that everyone sits in the office of a prophet (1 Cor. 12:28-31). Nevertheless, our attitude needs to be that of one who earnestly seeks these things in our lives (1 Cor. 14:1, 39).

Let's talk a little bit now about some practical methods you can use to help you hear God's voice in your life.[10]

As I shared earlier, I first began hearing God by journaling my Bible devotions. Habakkuk gives us a great example of how to position ourselves to do this:

> [1]*I will stand on my guard post And station myself on the rampart; And I will keep watch to see what He will speak to me, And how I may reply when I am reproved.* [2]*Then the LORD answered me and said, "Record the vision and inscribe it on tablets that the one who reads it may run"* (Habakkuk 2:1-2).

First, there is an attitude of hearing Him: "I will stand on my guard post And station myself on the rampart, And I will keep watch to see what He will speak to me." This is a positioning of ourselves to be looking. I call it the lost key syndrome.

Whenever you lose your keys, your whole world becomes myopic, focused on one thing: find those keys. One time I lost my keys and searched frantically for over two hours before I found them. It got to the point where I kept lifting the same couch pillows over and over again, hoping that somehow my keys would be there. Finally, in desperation, I had a brilliant idea: why not pray and ask the Lord where they are? I did that and then waited on Him. Soon I had a picture in my mind of a diaper pail. I have five daughters and they were little kids at the time, so I knew where that was. I went to the pail and started flinging out the rolled-up diapers. After going through about ten of them, I picked one up that felt light. I opened it up, and there were my keys!

In this exercise, like Habakkuk, you want to **position yourself** to hear from God. Like the lost keys, there needs to be a heart that says, like Elisha, "Where is the Lord God of Elijah?" (2 Ki. 2:14 NKJV)

Second, you want to **write out** what He says to you.

- Get something with which you feel comfortable recording what you hear, feel, or sense: a notebook or pad of paper, computer, iPad, or a voice recorder of some type.

- Find a place where you will have minimal distractions: no phone, no people, limited noise.
- If you want, play subtle worship music to help set the environment (Psalm 22:3 says that God is enthroned upon the praises of Israel).
- Take a moment and express your heart to the Lord in praise and worship.
- Ask the Lord, "What do you think of me?"

Record the thought, feeling, or emotion that you sense. The biggest obstacle to get through is the feeling that this is just you writing something down. In his book, *Is That Really You, God?* Lauren Cunningham talks about the tension of the still small voice (1Kings 19:11):

> Hearing God is not all that difficult. If we know the Lord, we have already heard His voice—after all, it was the inner leading that brought us to Him in the first place. But we can hear His voice once and still miss His best if we don't keep on listening. After the *what* of guidance come the *when* and the *how*.[11]

He later described a three-step model that he had learned for hearing God:

> We followed the Three Steps to Hearing God that I had first learned from Joy Dawson in New Zealand. First, we took Christ's authority to silence the enemy. Second, we asked the Lord to clear from our minds any presumptions and preconceived ideas. Third, we waited...believing He would speak in the way and in the time that He chose."[12]

The still small voice sounds like our voice; it is subtle, a hush in our heart. It can be a spontaneous thought, a hunch, a feeling, a sense of, or whatever language that resonates with you in hearing Him. As I said earlier, in any of the revelatory spiritual gifts in which you operate in, there is always the tension, is this me or is this God?

This is especially true with the prophetic and tongues. When you speak in a tongue, the Bible says your spirit prays but your mind is unfruitful (1 Cor. 14:14). Hearing your spirit pray does not resonate with your mind; to your mind is like speaking a foreign language. Your mind often will try to rationalize away what the Spirit is saying: "You are making this up. This is gibberish, and so cannot be of God."

In order to combat this, write out the first thought or impression that comes to your mind. Do not over-analyze or judge each thought. God speaks in these spontaneous random thoughts that we need to learn how to capture. I have found that people get stuck in this exercise when they try to overanalyze or over-think things. This is not Bible study; this is a conversation with God.

If you hear things like, "I love you, you are my chosen one," or "I delight in you," it most likely is the voice of God. How can I say this? Because it does not contradict the Word of God, and it is the Father heart of the Lord that He wants to express to you.

Maybe a scripture comes to your mind; record it. Perhaps the Lord gives you insight into a situation; record that. It is good to track the movements of the Holy Spirit in your life. Next, ask yourself, "How does it make me feel when I hear Him say this to me?"

Part of the problem of first hearing God's voice is that we have trained our minds and intellects but not our spirits. A recurrent theme in the Bible is to be still and to know that God is God. Psalm 4:4 says, "Tremble, and do not sin; Meditate in your heart upon your bed, and be still. Selah." Selah is a musical instruction to be silent or to pause for contemplation.

Two classic books I recommend that talk about eliminating distraction are, *The Interior Castle* by Teresa of Avila, and *Experiencing the Depths of God* by Jean Guyon. Both of these women lived in the 16th century, but their writings still encourage and inspire thousands of Christians today.[13]

If you find yourself distracted, reflect upon a scripture for a while. Tell your mind to be still and listen. Silence is one of the principal ways in which God communicates with us, so don't rush things. It is okay to be quiet; still yourself in His presence. If you are like most people, once you start to quiet yourself, your mind will start focusing on things other than hearing God. If this is the case, pull out your Bible, find one or two passages of scripture, and read them slowly over and over. This is biblical meditation, the process of slowing down and rehearsing a verse or promise of God. This is a very different practice than Bible reading. Most Western Christians are taught and encouraged to read the Bible, but few have been taught the importance of biblical meditation.

Notes

1 Craig S. Keener, *Gift & Giver: The Holy Spirit for Today*. (Grand Rapids: Baker Academic, a division of Baker Book House Company, 2001), 27.

2 Leland Ryken, Jim Wilhoit, Tremper Longman et al., *Dictionary of Biblical Imagery*, (Downers Grove: InterVarsity Press, 2000), 223, electronic ed.

3 Willard, *Hearing God*, 15.

4 Richard Whitaker et al., *The Abridged Brown-Driver-Briggs Hebrew-English Lexicon of the Old Testament: From A Hebrew and English Lexicon of the Old Testament by Francis Brown, S.R. Driver and Charles Briggs, Based on the Lexicon of Wilhelm Gesenius* (Boston; New York: Houghton, Mifflin and Company, 1906).

5 Lauren Cunningham, *Is That Really You, God?: Hearing the Voice of God*. YWAM Publishing; 2nd edition (June 1, 2001). This book is read by all YWAM DTS students and reinforces YWAM value number3, To hear His voice.

6 Willard, *Hearing God*.

7 Wayne Grudem, *The Gift of Prophecy in The New Testament and Today*, Revised edition. (Wheaton: Crossway, 2000). In his book, Grudem explains why hearing the voice of God does not add any new revelation to a closed canon and that hearing God's voice is a normative event for New Testament Christians today.

8 J. P. Moreland, quoted on https://worthlove.org/2014/06/29/furious-love-quotes, accessed March 4, 2019.

9 Apostle Jacquelyn Fedor, "Revelatory Gifts," http://www.trumpetsoftruth. com/lect_files/revelatory%20gifts.html, accessed March 4, 2019.

10 Mark and Patti Virkler have written a book that really touches on how to get started hearing God's voice: Mark and Patti Virkler, *4 Keys to Hearing God's Voice.* (Shippensburg: Destiny Image Publishers, 2010).

11 Cunningham, *Is That Really You, God?*, 11.

12 Cunningham, *Is That Really You, God?*, 142.

13 Jeanne Guyon, *Experiencing the Depths of Jesus Christ.* (Sargent: The Seed Sowers Christian Books Publishing House:1995) and Teresa of Avila, *The Interior Castle.* (London: Thomas Baker, 1921). Both of these books provide practical advice on quieting oneself before God. John Wesley and Watchman Nee both recommended Jeanne Guyon's book to their disciples.

Chapter Twelve

Hearing God for Others

"Why is it," comedian Lily Tomlin asks, "that when we speak to God we are said to be praying but when God speaks to us we are said to be schizophrenic?" Such a response from ourselves or others to someone's claim to have heard from God is especially likely today because of the lack of specific teaching and pastoral guidance on such matters.
                                                            – Dallas Willard[1]

It's a natural progression, as I shared in my testimony, to go from hearing God for yourself to hearing Him for others. This is the point where it becomes necessary to take some risks. If it helps you to relax with this idea, our identity should not be centered around how accurate we are in giving words, but around our heart as a child of God. The prophetic is about building others up, but there is a reciprocal blessing in this: as you give a word, the one in front of you receives a blessing and you receive a blessing in knowing that you heard God. Remember 1 Corinthians13:9: "For we know in part and we prophesy in part." That means that you usually don't get the whole download, so give what you got.

But one who prophesies strengthens others, encourages them, and comforts them (1 Corinthians 14:3 NLT).

For you can all prophesy one by one, so that all may learn and all may be exhorted (1 Corinthians 14:31).

²⁴But if all prophesy, and an unbeliever or an ungifted man enters, he is convicted by all, he is called to account by all; ²⁵the secrets of his heart are disclosed; and so he will fall on his face and worship God, declaring that God is certainly among you (1 Corinthians 14:24–25)

In this chapter we will practice hearing God's voice for others. When we talk about hearing God for others, the Bible calls this prophecy. Today, many refer to prophecy in terms of eschatology or the study of the end times. We need to let the Bible define the terms that we use. The Bible says that when we prophesy, the secrets of a man's heart are disclosed and he is convicted, and this will cause him to turn to God. In John 4, Jesus uses prophecy to disclose to the woman at the well his role as Messiah or the Christ. If Jesus used this method, shouldn't we?

When we hear God for others, it should fall under the context of 1 Corinthians 14:3, which states that a prophetic word should build, strengthen, and comfort the one we are giving it to. Wayne Grudem states, "prophecy is reporting in human words what God brings to mind."[2] New Testament prophecy differs from Old Testament prophecy in that Deuteronomy 18:20 says that if a prophet "misses it," he should be put to death. This was written for prophets who would minister to the kings of Israel. The New Testament says that we know in part, (we don't get the full picture), and we prophesy in part (share what knowledge we have). We are to judge prophetic words in the New Testament. That is to say, it's OK to say you missed it when giving a prophetic word (1 Corinthians13:9; 14:29).

The goal of your prophetic word is to bring life or the reality of Christ to a person so that they will acknowledge the Lord, and to help lead them in a deeper freedom and conviction of the Lord. There are a lot of different ways to start a prophetic word. The most vulnerable moment for a person is when they are just starting to prophesy. An early example of a Pentecostal prophetic delivery would go something like this: "Verily, verily, thus saith the Lord

Jesus…" and then the word would be given to the person. There are some problems with this delivery style.

First, it assumes that the word you are giving is 100 percent right on: "thus saith the Lord." First Corinthians 13 teaches us that we know in part and we prophesy in part and that we are to judge prophetic words. In the New Testament we are not 100 percent, in contrast to Deuteronomy 18, which said the prophet in the Old Testament had to be right 100 percent of the time. In the New Testament, we are to prophesy and let others pass judgement (1 Cor. 14:29). Why would we need to pass judgement if we are 100 percent? That is because we know only in part; we don't get the whole picture all the time (1 Cor.13:9). So, don't use this technique when starting off a word because it assumes that you are going to be 100 percent correct.

Second, it assumes that God speaks in "King James" language. Speak in a language that will be received by the one you are giving the word to. Don't talk down to anyone and don't dumb down the word you are giving. Look the person in the eye. Speak with compassion and passion when you give a word, but in a language they can understand. Learn to be naturally supernatural; be yourself and don't try to impress anyone.

One good way of delivering a prophecy is by saying, "I am sensing this." By stating that you are sensing something, it takes the pressure off of both you and God. If you start off by saying, "Thus said the Lord," you are leaving no room for error or interpretation. This older style of Pentecostal delivery method negates the word of God, which states that we know in part and we prophesy in part (1 Cor.13:9).

The second part, or the conclusion of your word, should be to ask the question, "Does that make sense to you?" This does two things. First, it gives you a sounding board to the accuracy or interpretation of the word. Sometimes, asking if it makes sense gives you a barometer for accuracy. You might have started out in the Spirit and then ended up in the flesh. You might have started out in the flesh and ended in the Spirit, or you might have started out in the flesh and ended in the flesh. So, this gives you some space to bring clarification or time to get the grace to say, "I missed it." Usually, if you started in the Spirit and landed in the Spirit, there will be a nodding of the head, tears, or a wide-eyed look on the person's face, followed by, "How did you know that?" Ending it with "Does that make sense?" gives the one delivering the word a confirmation that they are hearing God, which encourages them to continue prophesying.

It is vital to understand, if you miss it and the person says, "No that did not make any sense," that you don't get discouraged and say, "I will never do that again." Once, when I was ministering at a youth conference in Southern California, the Lord gave me a specific word for a young man. It was a detailed word regarding how many times his mom had been married, his own struggle for a father, and his drug addiction. When I asked him if it made sense he said, "No, dude, you are a nut case." My immediate reaction was to go into the corner of the room, grab a baby blanket, and start sucking my thumb. I heard my human heart say, "I will never do this again, but I could hear the Holy Spirit say, "Tell him I love him." So, I told him that the Lord loved him and longed for a relationship with him. He took off out of the room, and the next fifteen minutes were some of the longest in my life. Three of his friends came to me and said that everything that I had prophesied over him was correct, and he was up in his room telling everyone that he was going to do drugs until the day he died. My point here is this: do not get discouraged if you miss it. Respond with in humility. After all, it isn't about you; it's about God's crazy love for the person you are ministering to.

For example, I am a grandfather and I recently watched my grandson take his first steps. He had this big diaper and chubby little arms and legs. He held onto the coffee table as the whole family watched him. He had this big grin on his face as he let go of the coffee table. He started to wobble as he took his first steps. He made the first one okay, but fell on the second one. The whole room erupted in shouts of praise. I think this illustrates the Father heart of God for us as we step out into this realm. He cheers us, even though it might not be very pretty at first. If you suffer from rejection, don't get discouraged. We should try not to get an identity from how accurate we are, but in how loved we are by the Father.

Some prophetic people have a bent towards high revelatory words; they are very gifted in the prophetic. As Mike Bickle states in regard to prophetic words, "They are a mixture of God's words and man's words. Some 'prophetic words' may be 10 percent God's words and 90 percent man's words, while others have a greater revelatory content."³ For those who have a high degree of revelatory accuracy, the propensity to see sin or abuse is high. There is wisdom in delivering a prophetic word that will encourage a person rather than embarrass or humiliate them. For example, a person might discern sexual abuse. Instead of saying, "I see that you were molested by your stepfather when you were three," a better way would be to say, "I see that when you were young you went through some severe trauma." This speaks to the situation in the person's life without putting the prophetic accent on the abusive event but rather on how God is going to redeem it. Remember, a prophetic word needs to build, strengthen, and bring comfort. This is not to say that a corrective word is not to be given, but it needs to lead a person to hope of freedom (2 Cor. 3:11).

One example of this is Paul Cain, ⁴ an incredibly gifted prophet whose revelatory level was abnormally high and precise. I have personally seen him at the University of Irvine minister with John Wimber, and he would give people's names and home addresses when prophesying. When he was younger, Paul would call out people's sin in front of everyone. Needless to say, that method didn't work very well and the Lord had to give him wisdom regarding his delivery and developing a prophetic etiquette. One practical step in developing a prophetic etiquette is to ask the Lord, "What is it that I am sensing that you want me to say to this person that will build him up instead of cut them down?" Learn to wait, listen, and then speak. Sometimes the Lord might give you prophetic insight that is not to be disclosed. Therefore, in zeal to give a word, waiting and listening is the wisdom factor.

As you start to move in hearing God, the Lord will increase your ability to hear Him and to recognize His voice. Romans 12:6 says, "Since we have gifts that differ according to the grace given to us, *each of us is to exercise them accordingly*: if prophecy, according to the proportion of his faith." Your faith will grow as you use the gift. Consider it like a muscle; muscles atrophy when they aren't being used but grow strong when you exercise them. I like what *Easton's Bible Dictionary* says about exercise: "An ascetic mortification of the flesh and denial of personal gratification."[5] The flesh has got to die to our being right. Prophesying requires taking risks. John Wimber, the founder of the Vineyard movement said, "Faith is spelled RISK." "Little risks, little reward; great risks, great reward" should be our mantra if we want to grow in this.

There a few things that we should never step into when we prophesy. For example, I personally will never give a word as to whom one will marry, the name or sex of an unborn child, where one is to live, or what one is to be doing for a career. This might be personal prophetic preference, but if you are wrong, it can be manipulative to the one you are giving it to. Remember, you are to build, strengthen, and comfort with a prophetic word. You are not to direct, control, or manipulate with your prophetic words. Remember, as a general rule, no mates or dates.

Notes

1   Willard, *Hearing God*, 22.
2   Grudem, *The Gift of Prophecy in the New Testament and Today*, 51.
3   Mike Bickle, *Growing in the Prophetic*. (Lake Mary: Charisma House, 2008), 37.
4   Paul Cain, *The Life, Call and Ministry of Paul Cain. Voices from the Healing Revival Book 15*; Revival Library December 30, 2013. This book was published in 1950 but its copyright was never renewed. It is available in electronic format via Kindle.
5   M. G. Easton, *Easton's Bible Dictionary*. (New York: Harper & Brothers, 1893).

Chapter Thirteen

The Examen: Tracing the Move of the Holy Spirit Throughout Your Day

But what is so utterly foreign to many is the experience of falling in love with God. Religion, for them, is an intellectual exercise rooted in the individual conscience, rather than a response to a God who holds out a hand to say, "Let's have an adventure!"

–Timothy Muldoon[1]

The Examen is a prayer exercise that has been used for hundreds of years and is still used effectively today by multitudes of Christians who desire to stay in close contact with God. Originated by Ignatius of Loyola in the 1500s, the Examen helps us identify where God is throughout our day. Remember, God is always with us and promised never to leave us. Although it is very flexible, as a prayer exercise the Examen generally is more effective when done at the end of the day. Setting aside a quiet time of 10-20 minutes shortly before you go to bed, for example, would give you the opportunity to reflect with God on your day that has just ended to see where He has been at work. Thus, the Examen is a way to help you track the moving of the Holy Spirit in and around you throughout your day as well as help you remember that you are always in His presence.

Have you ever wondered on any given day where Jesus was in your life that day? The Examen helps you answer that question because it is a prayer of reflection. It is a prayer of looking back, not just at what went wrong during the day, which would be a narrow and potentially very harmful view, but a more general looking back at what you experienced, or where you were conscious of God at work that day.

In the Examen, the purpose is to observe without judging, to put you in the position where you can come into the presence of God and see more clearly how He has been moving and working in your life. It helps you focus on God, which is the purpose of the Examen, as with all prayer. This quiet focus on God enhances your ability to discern His presence and discover Him as He reveals himself to you in the everyday affairs of your life.

Every day is different: different moods, different activities, different experiences, different interactions with different people. Some days are calm and peaceful, others agitated and emotional. Some days are painful while others are nothing but pleasurable. Most days fall somewhere in between. No matter what kind of day you have had, the Examen helps you slow down, quiet your spirit, and acknowledge the presence of God, who normally comes to you and speaks to you in the quietness of your heart and mind.

As you become aware of God's presence, remember how good He has been to you and take a few moments to recall the many good gifts you have received from Him. Perhaps this very day God has shown His goodness to you and yours in a very special way. Meditate on that for a few minutes and realize that God's gifts and blessings to you demonstrate how deeply and thoroughly He loves you with an everlasting love.

As you review your day, ask God for the sensitivity of heart to see how He has been working in and through the events and circumstances of your day. Open yourself to allow God to give you the light, the spiritual insight that will enable you to see.

Practice looking at your day with gratitude no matter how it went. Beginning from the time you woke up in the morning, quietly review the events of the day. Remember that at this point you are not judging either yourself or others but simply looking calmly at your day as a neutral, objective observer. There are many ways of looking back. One helpful way is to ask yourself some questions. For example: On the whole, was it a good or bad day? Was it a normal day or was it unusual in some way? Who did I meet today? Did I come across something surprising? Did I run into an old friend? An old adversary? Did I do or see or hear something that stirred an old memory? A story? A beautiful sunset? Something I was told? Something I saw on television? A song or a piece of music? A piece of work or an activity of some kind? How did you feel as all these things were happening? Happy? Sad? Angry? Moody? Frightened? Peaceful? Contented? Did your feelings change during the day? If so, why? Who or what caused the change?

> God guides us through our moods and feelings. Normally the way of God is in a deep sense of peace and consolation. If your day was disturbed or you were uneasy, can you sense where that uneasiness was coming from. Like a sailor who is buffeted by many different winds, we are affected by many different feelings. The better we come to know these, the easier it will become to discern the subtle movement of God in our lives.[2]

Another important question to ask yourself is, "What can I be proud of today?" There will always be something! If you can't think of anything, you haven't looked hard enough. Ask God to show you. Don't move on before you can affirm something encouraging.

In a change of focus, ask yourself whether you have turned away from God in any way during the day, or turned a blind eye to His movement in yourself or others. This may be painful, but don't skip over it. Deal honestly with it before yourself and God. Remember, He is a God of mercy. In your own words, confess and ask forgiveness for anything you may have done to ignore or hinder God during the day. Ask for healing grace and strength.

The final part of the prayer of Examen is to look forward to tomorrow. What will happen when the new day dawns? Will there be times when it will be especially good to see the presence of God? Christians are people of hope; whatever the new day may bring, pray for the sensitivity to see God's presence in the daily routine of your life.

> If we practice the Examen, we will grow to know ourselves, our moods and with the help of God, see in our prayer the way that God is moving in our lives. As our hearts become more sensitive we will recognize God more quickly so that eventually we will be sensitive to the God who is not just in 'holy' things, but the God who is in all things.[3]

Notes

1   Timothy Muldoon, quoted by George Aschenbrenner in the Foreword to Timothy M. Gallagher, *The Examen Prayer: Ignatian Wisdom for Our Lives Today*. (New York: The Crossroad Publishing Company, 2006).

2   https://www.stgeorgesparis.com/worship-with-us/lent-holy-week-and-easter-2019, accessed March 8, 2019.

3   https://www.stgeorgesparis.com/worship-with-us/lent-holy-week-and-easter-2019.

Chapter Fourteen

How to Operate in the Miraculous

For many Charismatics, Scripture is not simply a book to be read and studied, but it is an invitation into a lifestyle of supernatural engagement. Truly, such followers of Jesus desire to be doers of the Word, not hearers only. This should be celebrated rather than rejected.

–Randy Clark[1]

I used to pray for the sick by voicing a simple, casual prayer and then walking away. At that time, my thought was, "If God heals them, then He heals them." Since then, I have learned a better way so that today I witness healings on a fairly regular basis, as does my church body as we practice this. In this chapter I want to give you some practical approaches so that you too can operate in the miraculous in your life.

Where healing is concerned, a word of knowledge can be the easiest mode to operate in. Remember, a word of knowledge is a revelatory gift that involves hearing the voice of God. A friend of mine who works at the International House of Prayer in Pasadena, California once asked me, "Nick, you are gifted in hearing God. Do you see many miracles?" I told him that no one had ever really taught me how to do that. "All you have to do is pray," he said, "and the Lord will tell you who He is going to heal." John 16:13 is the premise for this; the Holy Spirit will tell us of things to come.

I thought to myself, "Little risk, little reward; great risks, great reward. Why not try this?"

Just before church the following Sunday morning, I asked the Lord who He wanted to heal. I felt like I heard Him, "There are two women here with autoimmune diseases whom I want to heal." So, I called it out in our 9 a.m. service. I said, "I feel like there are two women out there today who have autoimmune diseases. If that is you, would you please stand up." Two women stood up. Thank you, Jesus! One of them I recognized, but the other was a first-time visitor to our church. One of the cardinal rules for pastors is never to embarrass a first-time visitor, and yet I asked her to stand up. When she did, she looked at her friend and said, "What's up with this?" Her friend was trying to console her and let her know that I was just praying for her, but again she asked, "What's up with this?" She was dead center in the second row, so everyone in the congregation could see what was happening. "This was a bad idea," I said to myself. "I will never do this again."

Suddenly, the woman spoke again. "Why did they turn the air conditioner on?" Her friend told her they hadn't. "Then, why is there wind blowing all over my body?" In that instant she was healed from Crohn's disease, and I will always remember her name. Her name is Windy, and today Windy is still serving Jesus. You can get a word of knowledge simply by asking the Lord what or who He wants to touch.

The ministry of healing always carries the tension of why certain people get healed and others don't. Classical Pentecostal theology teaches that healing is in the atonement, the redemptive work that Jesus did on the cross.

⁴Surely our griefs He Himself bore, And our sorrows He carried; Yet we ourselves esteemed Him stricken, Smitten of God, and afflicted. ⁵But He was pierced through for our transgressions, He was crushed for our iniquities; The chastening for our well-being fell upon Him, And by His scourging we are healed (Isaiah 53:4–5).

Most Christians agree that Jesus died on the cross for our sins. Many of them, however, do not know or believe that He also purchased our healing there. Over one-third of the public ministry of Jesus recorded in the Gospels was devoted to healing. If this is so, shouldn't ours be as well? If healing is in the atonement, then why doesn't everyone get healed? Here's the logic, if you look at Isaiah 53: Christians believe that Jesus died for our sins and that He desires that none perish. Does that mean that everyone we pray for gets saved? Of course not, but we know that we still are to do the work of the evangelist and try to bring people into the kingdom of God.

If you take credit for someone getting healed, then you need to take credit when someone doesn't get healed. Why is it that some people are healed and others aren't? Some teach that it is because of lack of faith. Then the question becomes, "How much faith is enough?" Or put another way, "How little faith is too little?" Jesus said that faith the size of a grain of mustard seed can move mountains, so lack of faith does not seem to be the answer. One long-standing and widely-held religious tradition claims that God often sends sickness, oppression, and other afflictions to teach us a lesson. The problem with this claim is that no such teaching is found in the Bible. That idea is a tradition of man trying to deal with the issue of theodicy (why bad things happen to good people, or the defense of God's goodness in the midst of evil). Paul had his thorn in the flesh, but was that a disease sent from God? We need to read things in context whenever we read the Bible: "even though I have received such wonderful revelations from God. So to keep me from becoming proud, I was given a thorn in my flesh, **a messenger from Satan** to torment me and keep me from becoming proud (2 Cor. 12:7 NLT, emphasis added).

Paul makes it clear that his thorn was *a messenger from Satan.* This is completely consistent with Ezekiel 2:6: "And you, son of man, be not afraid of them, nor be afraid of their words, though briers and thorns are with you and you sit on scorpions. Be not afraid of their words, nor be dismayed at their looks, for they are a rebellious house" (ESV). In Ezekiel's case, God was sending him to the house of Israel, where he would find a rebellious people.

The false messengers of Satan among the children of Israel, whom God calls thorns and scorpions, is the same symbolism that we find with Paul's thorn in the flesh. The thorn imagery in Ezekiel is completely consistent with a messenger of Satan berating the apostle Paul, and totally inconsistent with understanding the thorn as an illness or physical debilitation.

Scripture teaches that God is good—and only good—all the time (Ps. 34:8; 100:5; 135:3; 145:9). It also teaches that God is immutable; that is, He never changes (Mal. 3:6; Heb. 13:8). When God finished creating the world and everything in it, including mankind, He surveyed everything He had made and pronounced it "very good" (Gen. 1:31). Only good things come from God because He is absolute goodness. How then could sickness and other afflictions in the world originate with God, who is perfect goodness and perfect love? He sent His Son to redeem us from the curse of sin and all its consequences.

If you take the claim that God sends sickness to its logical (but skewed) conclusion, you have this: "It's God's will that these people are sick, so if I pray for them to get well I am praying against God's will." So, how do you know who to pray for, then, if God wills some people to be sick? This dilemma could easily lead many people to stop praying for anyone to be healed for fear of going against God, who might want the sick people in that condition. Following this logic to its natural conclusion would lead people not to pray for anyone to be healed because of not knowing whether or not God wants them in that condition.

If God did not send sickness to the earth, how did it get here? Where did it come from? It came from Satan. Sickness entered into the human experience along with sin in the garden of Eden. Adam and Eve's sin afflicted the whole earth with a curse and opened the door to illness, strife, misery, and death. Created by God as co-regents with authority to rule over the created realm, Adam and Eve abdicated their authority to a deceitful, lying usurper. From that day until this, that usurper, Satan, whom Paul calls the "god of this world" (2 Cor. 4:4), and Jesus, the "prince of this world" (Jn. 12:31; 14:30; 16:11) has dominated human affairs. Satan was delegated authority in the earth by man's disobedience. I often wonder why Adam and Eve did not recognize the authority they had been given. We do not want to make that same mistake in regard to knowing our authority as believers. Matthew 28:18 says, "And Jesus came and said to them, 'All authority in heaven and on earth has been given to me'" (ESV). Jesus, by His atoning work at Calvary, has been given back the authority that Satan usurped; it's part of the victory of Calvary. Jesus said, "Behold, I have given you authority to tread on serpents and scorpions, and **over all the power of the enemy**, and nothing shall hurt you" (Lk. 10:19 ESV, emphasis added). Jesus has given us all power over the enemy. Why? So we can attest to His triumphant kingdom (Acts 2:22). For a limited time, only until Jesus returns, Satan pretty much rules the roost on earth, especially over the lost, and, to a lesser degree, believers who do not understand that in Christ they have complete authority over him.

Right now a clash of two kingdoms is going on. In *God at War*, author Gregory Boyd writes:

> This is our part in spiritual war. We proclaim Christ's truth by praying it, speaking it and (undoubtedly most importantly) by demonstrating it. We are not to accept with pious resignation the evil aspects of our world as "coming from a father's hand." Rather, following the example of our Lord and Savior, and going forth with the confidence that he has in principle already defeated his (and our) foes, we are to revolt against the evil aspects of our world as coming from the devil's hand. Our revolt is to be broad--as broad as the evil we seek to confront, and as broad as the work of the cross we seek to proclaim. Wherever there is destruction, hatred, apathy, injustice, pain or hopelessness, whether it concerns God's creation, a structural feature of society, or the physical,

psychological or spiritual aspect of an individual, we are in word and deed to proclaim to the evil powers that be, "You are defeated." As Jesus did, we proclaim this by demonstrating it."[2]

Too many people, and, tragically, far too many Christians, mistakenly believe that God is the author and sender of sickness and other tragedies in the world. This stands in complete contradiction to what the Bible teaches.

Again, Gregory Boyd:

> If we further consider this divine panoramic view within which all evil is supposedly a "secret good" is held by a God who, according to Scripture, has a passionate hatred toward all evil, the "solution" becomes more problematic still. For it is certainly not clear how God could hate what he himself wills and sees as a contributing ingredient in the good of the whole.[3]

God continually takes the hit from people for the miseries Satan inflicts on the earth. Jesus said that, unlike a thief or robber, who comes only to steal, kill, and destroy, He came to give abundant life (Jn. 10:10). How can sickness bring abundant life to anyone? If we pray the Lord's prayer, "Thy kingdom come, thy will be done on earth as it is in heaven," the question arises, "Is there any sickness in heaven?" The answer is no.

If you want to understand the will of God concerning healing, just look at Jesus. He is the perfect picture of God the Father. He made this clear when He said, "I and the Father are one" (Jn. 10:30), and "He who has seen Me has seen the Father" (Jn. 14:9b). Jesus always did the Father's will and only the Father's will: "For I have come down from heaven, not to do My own will, but the will of Him who sent Me" (Jn. 6:38), and "I do nothing on My own initiative, but I speak these things as the Father taught Me" (Jn. 8:28b). In the synagogue in Nazareth one Sabbath early in His ministry, Jesus read from Isaiah: [18]"The Spirit of the Lord is upon me, because he has anointed me to proclaim good news to the poor. He has sent me to proclaim liberty to the captives and recovering of sight to the blind, to set at liberty those who are oppressed, ¹⁹to proclaim the year of the Lord's favor" (Lk. 4: 18-19 ESV). If Jesus did only the Father's will, what was it Jesus did? He healed the sick, raised the dead, cast out demons, restored sight to the blind, hearing to the deaf, and released those under spiritual oppression. Jesus' very example shows us very clearly how God feels about every human affliction and tragedy.

Matthew 4 gives us a picture of the earliest days of Jesus' public ministry. After fasting for 40 days in the wilderness and triumphing over Satan's temptations, Jesus established a base of operations in Capernaum, called the first four of His disciples, and began to preach "Repent, for the kingdom of heaven is at hand," (Mt. 4:17). Then he began traveling as an itinerant teacher, and we get a glimpse of how He ministered in Galilee:

> ²³*Jesus traveled throughout the region of Galilee, teaching in the synagogues and announcing the Good News about the Kingdom. And he healed every kind of disease and illness.* ²⁴*News about him spread as far as Syria, and people soon began bringing to him all who were sick. And whatever their sickness or disease, or if they were demon possessed or epileptic or paralyzed—he healed them all* (Matthew 4:23–24 NLT).

In Matthew 10, Jesus called His twelve disciples together and delegated to them His preaching and healing authority:

> ¹*Jesus called his twelve disciples together and gave them authority to cast out evil spirits and to heal every kind of disease and illness…* ⁷*Go and announce to them that the Kingdom of Heaven is near.* ⁸*Heal the sick, raise the dead, cure those with leprosy, and cast out demons. Give as freely as you have received!* (Matthew 10:1, 7-8 NLT)

The Greek word for "authority" in verse one is ἔξεστιν, *exousia*, which means, "It is free." It denotes that an action is possible in the sense that there are no hindrances or that the opportunity for it occurs, i.e., "to have the possibility," "to be able."⁴ Jesus gave *exousia* to His disciples to do the miraculous. It was possible and they were now able to do it because He gave them authority.

The Gospel of Mark also speaks of this miraculous power given to Jesus' followers:

> ¹⁷*"And these signs will accompany those who believe: in my name they will cast out demons; they will speak in new tongues;* ¹⁸*they will pick up serpents with their hands; and if they drink any deadly poison, it will not hurt them; they will lay their hands on the sick, and they will recover"* (Mark 16:17–18 ESV).

Is it God's will for people to be healed? Jesus healed many people and plainly said that He did only His Father's will. So, then, is it God's will for people to be healed? Just ask the former leper who approached Jesus one day and said, "Lord, if you are willing, you can make me clean," to whom Jesus replied, "I am willing"—and then healed him (Mt. 8:1-3). Is it God's will for people to be healed? Just ask the formerly disabled woman who spent 18 years bent over, unable to straighten herself fully, until the day Jesus saw her, called her over, laid His hands on her, and freed her from her disability. Standing straight for the first time in 18 years, she immediately began praising God (Lk. 13:11-13). Is it God's will for people to be healed? Just ask the formerly blind man who called out to Jesus as He was leaving Jericho and said, "Jesus, Son of David, have mercy on me!" When Jesus called him over and asked, "What do you want Me to do for you?", the man replied, "I want to regain my sight," and Jesus granted his request (Mk. 10:46-52).

So, then does sickness come from God, or does *victory over* sickness come from God? One modern-day healing evangelist answers the question this way:

It is not possible for me to accept the teaching that sickness comes from God as I follow the Ministry of Jesus through the Bible. Some people insist that God makes people sick because their preacher or their home Church believes it that way. I don't care what some mis-informed preacher says. I want to know what the Bible says.

- The Bible says that God anointed Jesus with power to force back Satan in people's lives. (Acts 10:38)
- The Bible says God is the Blesser and Satan is the damner. (John 10:10)
- The Bible says that Jesus came to do His Father's will and He always healed people. (John 6:38)
- The Bible says that God was the One performing the healing miracles through Jesus. (John 14:10)
- The Bible reveals that Jesus corrected a sick man for questioning whether He would heal him or not. (Matthew 8:3)
- The Bible reveals that Satan binds and Jesus looses. (Luke 13:6)

By following the Ministry of Jesus in action, we see the will of God in action.

So, what do you say? Do you say what the Bible says or do you believe what tradition and religion and the devil say? If you believe the Bible and need healing in your body, God will heal you. Do you belong to His Family? If not, just say, "Jesus, You're my choice." (Romans 10:13) You'll be immediately transferred into the Family of God and qualify for the benefit of healing. (Colossians 1:12, 13)[5]

We need to understand why Jesus came to earth. Jesus came to earth to seek and to save the lost, to testify to the truth, and to destroy the works of the devil.

- He came to seek the lost: "For the Son of Man came to seek and to save what was lost" (Lk. 19:10 NIV).
- He came to testify to the truth: "'You are a king, then!' said Pilate. Jesus answered, 'You are right in saying I am a king. In fact, for this reason I was born, and for this I came into the world, to testify to the truth. Everyone on the side of truth listens to me'" (Jn. 18:37 NIV).

- He came to destroy the works of the devil: "He who does what is sinful is of the devil, because the devil has been sinning from the beginning. The reason the Son of God appeared was to destroy the devil's work" (1 Jn. 3:8 NIV).
- He came to destroy death: "Since the children have flesh and blood, he too shared in their humanity so that by his death he might destroy him who holds the power of death—that is, the devil—and free those who all their lives were held in slavery by their fear of death" (Heb 2:14-15 NIV).

Sickness does not come from God; it is one of the consequences of sin. Victory over sickness comes from God and is part of Christ's completed work on the cross. In fact, the healing aspect of Jesus' ministry is inseparably linked to His atonement:

> Christ died to reverse the curse resulting from the sin of our first parents; He redeemed us from the curse of the Law (Galatians 3:13). The curse was death — both physical and spiritual. He died for the whole man, not only for man's soul. His redemptive work includes salvation for all aspects of man's being, however one conceives the interrelationship of body, soul, and spirit.
>
> Physical healing occurs as a result of the atoning work of Christ, but at best it is only a temporary deliverance since all must die. The greater physical deliverance is the redemption of the body, which will undergo not only resurrection but also transformation, never again to be subject to sickness and disease (Romans 8:23; Philippians 3:20,21). Ultimately, the consequences of physical and spiritual death have been overcome by the death of the One who took upon himself both our sins and our sicknesses.[6]

A Five-Step Model for Healing

In concluding this chapter, I want to give you a procedure for praying for the sick that will help you linger longer and not just pray a prayer and go on. John Wimber, the founder of the Vineyard

Movement, led healing conferences around the world and his teaching impacted thousands of Christians in the 20th century. He once told about receiving cards or letters from numerous people who had sat under his teaching who shared a similar disappointment, saying something to the effect of, "I went home and prayed for somebody and it didn't work." John's serious but lighthearted reply: "Why don't you pray for a thousand somebodies, and then let's talk." John Wimber regularly used a five-step model for healing. This model has been used to train thousands around the world today. Randy Clark, the founder of Global Awakening, uses John's five-step model to train people all around the world in how to minister healing.

> At its essence, the 5-Step Prayer Model is a relational, interactive way of praying for others as we listen to the Holy Spirit – a process that begins and ends with mercy toward the person requesting prayer, and that seeks both God's will and God's best for the person being prayed for. It is also relational in the sense that we are leaning heavily on our intimate relationship with God as we pray, welcoming Him to speak insights into our heart or mind that would directly impact the person being prayed for.[7]

I have seen Randy Clark use this method as a primary training mode for equipping believers. What impresses me most about Randy is not the model but, the love he has for the one he is praying for.[8]

John Wimber has noted the versatility of the five-step model:

> The five-step procedure may be used any time and in any place: in hotels, at neighbor's homes, on airplanes, at the office, and, of course, in church gatherings. I have been in casual conversation with people, even with complete strangers, who mention some physical condition, and I ask, 'May I pray for you?' Rarely do they decline healing prayer, even if they are not Christians. I then confidently pray for them by following the five-step method"[9]

There are different ways of praying for the sick. The following five-step model is not the only one. If you have found one that is effective for you, use it in your own personal ministry.

This five-step model is used by Randy Clark and ministry teams at Global Awakening crusades and events. It is quiet, loving and effective. It can be used by anyone.[10]

The five steps are:

1. *The Interview*
2. *Prayer Selection*
3. *Prayer Ministry*
4. *Stop and Re-interview*
5. *Post-prayer Suggestions*

The interview is a series of questions: "What is your name?" "What is going on with your body?" "How long have you had this condition?" What would you like prayer for?"

Prayer selection is deciding what type of prayer they need; Petition or Command. **Petition:** A request to heal, addressed to God, to Jesus, or to the Holy Spirit. **Command:** A command addressed to a condition of the body, or to a part of the body, or to a troubling spirit such as a spirit of pain, infirmity, or affliction.

Prayer ministry is the act of praying for the person. Ask the person not to pray while you are praying for him. Here again, be gentle and loving. Say something like: "I know this means a lot to you, and you have probably prayed a lot about your condition. But for now, I need you to focus on your body. I want you to just relax and let me know if anything begins to happen in your body, like heat, tingling, electricity, a change in the amount or location of the pain, etc." If you sense it, lead the person in forgiveness if someone has wronged them. They might need to repent for their own behavior.

Ask them if there has been any effect upon them. It is often very helpful to pray with your eyes open so you can observe the person you are praying for. Look for signs that God is at work in his body: fluttering eyelids, trembling, perspiration. If you see something happening or if the person reports a change in the pain or increased sight or other progress, thank God for what He is doing and bless it. Continue to pray in the manner that led to the progress.

If you are not accustomed to praying with your eyes open, this will require practice! So many people think they have to pray with their eyes closed because that is the only way God can hear them. "God, I have my eyes closed now; can you hear me?" God can hear you with your eyes open. You want your eyes open so that you can see what is going on with the person in front of you. It is worth the practice of keeping your eyes open so you won't miss what God is doing.

Use your normal tone of voice. Shouting or praying loudly in tongues will not increase your effectiveness. Don't preach, don't give advice, and don't prophesy. STAY THE COURSE with the prayer for healing. We have been taught that God always heals immediately, but that is not what the Bible teaches. In Mark 8, Jesus prayed for a blind man to be healed, and it took Him several rounds of prayer before healing was accomplished. If Jesus needs to pray several times, perhaps we do as well.

> [23]*And he took the blind man by the hand and led him out of the village, and when he had spit on his eyes and laid his hands on him, he asked him, "Do you see anything?"* [24]*And he looked up and said, "I see people, but they look like trees, walking."* [25]*Then Jesus laid his hands on his eyes again; and he opened his eyes, his sight was restored, and he saw everything clearly* (Mark 8:23–25 ESV).

Remember, this is a model, not a formula. Use it as a guide when you're not sure what to do!

Step 1: The Interview. "Where does it hurt?" or "What would you like me to pray for?" Introduce yourself. Natural level: what can you see? Supernatural: ask God for words of knowledge, discernment, visions. This is not a medical interview; get the facts. Move to the next stage when ready: you know the cause, or God tells you to.

Step 2: The Diagnosis. Why do they have this condition? Natural causes: disease; accident; sin, either committed by them or against them; emotional hurts causing physical or other pain; relationship problems; lack of forgiveness. Supernatural causes: perhaps demonic. Keep asking for God's help. It may be useful to pray in tongues. Ask them questions, if appropriate.

Step 3: Prayer Selection. What kind of prayer shall I pray to help this person? Ask the Holy Spirit to come and minister to the person's body. Lay on hands and ask for God to heal. Keep praying in the Spirit. Command—of faith (Acts 3:6). Pronouncement—of faith (Jn. 4:50). Demonic—rebuke (break their power); bind them (contain); expel (get rid of).

Step 4: Prayer Engagement. "How are you doing?" Watch for the effects – keep your eyes open! Phenomenological signs—(warmth, tingling, shaking etc.). Ask questions—find out what God is doing. Stop when—they think it's all over, the Spirit tells you it's over, you've run out of things to pray, or when it's going nowhere. Remove your hands and talk to them to indicate you are stopping

Step 5: Post-prayer Direction. Encourage them to read their Bibles, spend time with God, get involved or stay involved in the local church, and check with their doctor. If they're not healed, reassure them that God loves them and encourage them to keep on asking and getting prayer until they are finished or have to leave.

Notes

1   Randy Clark, *The Essential Guide to the Power of the Holy Spirit: God's Miraculous Gifts at Work Today.* (Shippensburg: Destiny Image Publishers, 2015).

2   Gregory A. Boyd, *God at War: The Bible and Spiritual Conflict.* (Downer's Grove: InterVarsity Press, 1997). In this book Gregory Boyd undertakes to re-look at issues of Christian theodicy. By Boyd's estimate, theologians still draw

too heavily on Augustine's response to the problem of evil, attributing pain and suffering to the mysterious "good" purposes of God.

3   Boyd, *God at War*.

4   Werner Foerster, "Ἔξεστιν, Ἐξουσία, Ἐξουσιάζω, Κατεξουσιάζω," ed. Gerhard Kittel, Geoffrey W. Bromiley, and Gerhard Friedrich, *Theological Dictionary of the New Testament* (Grand Rapids, MI: Eerdmans, 1964–), 560.

5   http://www.johnhamelministries.org/sickness_not_from_God.htm, accessed March 15, 2019.

6   Anthony D. Palma, "Healing and the Atonement," http://enrichment-journal.ag.org/Tools_of_the_Trade/article_display.cfm?targetBay=d-8fa2daa-0f05-4f8b-b3e8-f65bba19df5b&ModID=2&Process=DisplayArticle&RSS_RSSContentID=6256&RSS_OriginatingChannelID=1170&RSS_OriginatingRSSFeedID=3344&RSS_Source=, accessed March 15, 2019.

7   https://www.vineyardchurches.org.uk/tools/5-step-model-of-healing/, accessed March 15, 2019.

8   I got my D. Min with Randy Clark and have had opportunities to pray for the sick with him. Once we prayed for a professor at our seminary who had cancer. Randy spent over an hour praying for this woman. I learned more by watching his compassion than I did from anything else that day.

9   John Wimber and Kevin Springer, *Power Healing*. (New York: HarperCollins, 1987). Quoted at https://www.vineyardchurches.org.uk/tools/5-step-model-of-healing/, accessed March 15, 2019.

10 Clark, Randy, *Ministry Team Training Manual* (Apostolic Network of Global Awakening, Mechanicsburg, PA. 2004).

Chapter Fifteen

Becoming a Word and Spirit Church

"My speech and my message were not in plausible words of wisdom, but in demonstration of the Spirit and of power" (1 Corinthians 2: 4). In the same letter he wrote, "For the kingdom of God does not consist in talk but in power," and he speaks of the Holy Spirit giving "the working of miracles" (1 Corinthians 4: 20; 12: 10)."

– Randy Clark[1]

In chapter one I acknowledged the cultural shift we are in the midst of today. If you are a baby boomer, there is a high chance that you have a modernist mindset: facts are reality, absolute truth can be determined, and a logical and rational mindset is valuable. It requires a massive paradigm shift for a modernist to rely on feelings as a guide for truth, as the metamodernist does today. If you are a postmodernist, you believe that there are no absolute truths and that feelings determine reality. As far back as 1979, excellent apologists like Josh McDowell gave us logical reasons why the Bible is true. Because of his classic work *Evidence that Demands a Verdict*, we as Christians can be sure that the life, death, burial, and resurrection of Jesus, are actual historical events. We can count on the inerrancy of the scriptures that we have today. This was the apologetic for reaching the lost: give them logical explanations for the reliability of the Gospel accounts. As an argument in defense of Christianity, it has a modernist appeal.[2] I believe traditional apologetics is needed today for metamodernists, but they first must have an experience that touches their emotions. The apologetic for reaching this generation requires an experience that touches their heart, leads them to Jesus, and then disciples them in a traditional apologetic, giving them reasons to believe.

As Norman Geisler writes:

> Anyone who claims to be God in human flesh needs to offer sufficient validations if he expects people to believe him. This is exactly what Jesus does. A key component of Christ's apologetic is the miraculous signs that he performs to substantiate his claim.[3]

A little later, he defines miracles:

> Natural laws describe what occurs regularly by natural causes, but miracles are special acts of God that interrupt the normal course of events and confirm the Word of God through a messenger of God."[4]

We can run into all sorts of issues when we rely strictly on our feelings. Basing our faith too much on the experiential can become problematic, especially if we have to go through any suffering for the gospel's sake. I have seen young revivalists who are amazingly gifted and can demonstrate the power of God, but who never open their Bibles. The biggest problem with this is what it does to the next generation. For example, the seeker-sensitive movement, as noted earlier in the book, has failed to make grounded disciples. You have to say the hard things and convince people to count the costs. The gospel cannot be consumer-driven; it must be kingdom-driven.

Alan Hirsch has written about the consumer-driven church in America and its irrelevance in other parts of the world.[5] In a consumer-driven church, Sunday becomes the show. It's about who has the best worship program, kids' program, and youth program in town. He calls consumer-driven church "Little Jesus in Disneyland." It's about the entertainment of the people over the Lordship of Jesus.

When we don't open our Bibles, and base our Christianity only on experiences, we run into trouble. Remember Acts 2:22, which says that signs, wonders, and miracles are to attest to Jesus, not to our gift. Whenever we demonstrate the power of God without pointing people to God, the charismata becomes all about us. We can try to rationalize this away by saying that we gave this person a spiritual encounter, but what spirit? I see this leading to a type of Christian spiritualism, an experience without a doctrine.

There are many people today who consider themselves "spiritual," but who have or follow no particular doctrine. At the Royal Television Society Awards in England in 2015, a program entitled *Exploring the Unexplained* won the award as best documentary. It also was nominated as the best documentary at London's International Film Awards. People were hungry for the supernatural; they were amazed at the reality of the spiritual realm, but no one was led to Jesus. We can run into the same problem if we present Jesus with signs, wonders, and miracles, but don't point people to Him.

Selwyn Stevens addresses the problems related to spiritualism in an online article entitled, "Spiritualism: A Christian Perspective":

What can we say about Spiritualism?

First, it is selfish and self-centred, as people seek for what they can get out of it, rather than serving or giving to others. One commentator described Spiritualism as attempting to obtain heavenly superannuation on easy terms.

Second, it is materialistic, seeking a type of heaven which is very earthly and rather limited. One could agree with the comment that it's a case of tired spirits in search of a spa. The supposed afterlife of the spiritualist seems very close to the old Scandinavian concept of Valhalla, or perhaps even the Moslem's paradise.

Third, the revelations by these spirits tell nothing about God, so it is untheological. The God of the Bible is the only reputable guarantee of the survival of the human soul after death, yet this is barely mentioned by Spiritualists.[6]

In 1987, a Miller Lite commercial rag about their new lite beer with the tagline, "It tastes great, but it's less filling." Prior to this commercial, the general opinion among beer drinkers was that no lite beer could taste good and be less filling; it had to be one or the other. A similar reality characterizes many churches today: they are either all Bible and no Spirit, or all Spirit and no Bible. The new covenant promise was of Word *and* Spirit, that people would know God's Word deep within them, that it would go from the head right to the heart, and that they would be empowered to live righteously by the indwelling of the Spirit.

Too often the disunion between Word and Spirit churches is a vast chasm of doctrinal differences. A church might be known for its doctrinal correctness and strong Word, or noted for the presence and moving of the Spirit. Chuck Smith, the founding pastor of the Calvary Chapel movement, once said, "Too much Word we dry up, too much Spirit we blow up. Just enough Word and just enough Spirit, we grow up." It's time that we grow up and utilize all of our God-given resources to reach this world for Jesus. That great task entails that we be people of the Word who also demonstrate God's power to a lost world, not just talk about His power.

In Matthew 22:29, Jesus corrects the Sadducees, who had challenged Him about the resurrection of the dead. The Sadducees were the priests who were in charge of all the Temple services. Their point of reference was the Pentateuch, the first five books of the Bible, of which they had a highly-developed doctrine. But they did not accept the rest of the scriptures and had little use for the supernatural. For this reason, they did not believe in the resurrection of the dead. But Jesus set them straight: "You are wrong, because you know neither the scriptures nor the power of God" (ESV). That word "know," you will remember, is *ginosko* in the Greek and refers to a type of knowing by experience or revelation. Jesus rebuked the Sadducees because they did not know (by experience or revelation) the *dunamis* (dynamic) power of God. The Sadducees had their doctrine down pat, but they didn't understand (or even believe in) God's power.

Essentially, Jesus told these experts in the Word that they didn't know the Word. Imagine the outrage these proud scholars must have felt when Jesus declared their ignorance. For them, the power of God was a great enigma, something that wasn't even on their radar. They had come to debate the Law, not talk about supernatural power, but Jesus made the two inseparable; it was He who brought it up, not them. The power of God was totally irrelevant to them. Sometimes I wonder if it is the same way with many Christians and some of our churches today: "I know my Bible. I have a well-developed doctrine and major theological degrees; what does the Spirit have to do with anything?" My point here is that, for Jesus, knowing His Word correlates to knowing His power. The scriptures and the power of God are inseparable.[7]

Word and Spirit can mean different things to different people. Some argue that they are Word and Spirit, but in application it doesn't look that way. The gifts need to be sought and used so that people will know the reality of Christ. In that same context, we need to be students of the Bible. Watchman Nee said, "There is another thing that the Holy Spirit does and this concerns the Word of God. Many people do not see the relationship between the Holy Spirit and the Word of God. Hence, they do not treasure the words of the Bible that much."[8]

Paul counseled Timothy to "Do your best to present yourself to God as one approved, a worker who has no need to be ashamed, rightly handling the word of truth" (2 Tim. 2:15 ESV). As people who embrace Word and Spirit, we need to work on our grasp of scripture so that we can handle the Word of truth rightly. We cannot handle things rightly if we are ignorant of biblical truth. I am not saying that we need to be theologians, but we need to be diligent students of the Bible. Our mantra should be, "The Bible says…" I know that today's culture no longer recognizes the Bible as a source of authority, but that is no excuse for us not using the Word of God when we minister.

Some say that the discipleship model of Jesus looks like this: I do while you watch, you do while I watch, and then you go and do while someone else watches. The problem with this logic is that they forget to ask the question, "What was Jesus doing?" He was healing the sick, raising the dead, casting demons out of people, and reading the scriptures in the local synagogue.

Gary Grieg says, " Jesus' message and ministry are one."[9] R. H. Fuller sees the homogenizing of Christ's message this way: "...the miracles of Jesus are part and parcel of his kerygmatic activity. In fact, the miracles are part of the proclamation itself, quite as much as the spoken words of Jesus."[10] In Jesus' kingdom, He has authority over the demonic, and over sickness and disease, and He delegates His authority to His disciples. Jon Ruthven says, "Our job is to emulate Jesus and His ministry in the power of the Spirit."[11] But we also need to emulate Him in His high regard of the scriptures.

Ruthven establishes a lens through which believers are to look at scripture. This is excellently illustrated by his "Traditionalist Filter" dialogue, where he makes the point that when one reads the scripture under the traditional method there is an automatic filter that tells one; "God cannot speak directly to me today".[12] There is a theological conditioning that convinces us to believe that we cannot do the things that were done in the Bible. This is a key point to his book. "We can do the things that are mentioned in the Bible today." Ruthven states that "the New Covenant is the goal of the Bible and that taking the form of the bestowal of the Spirit upon man."[13] We need to rethink how we equip people for ministry.[14] His approach brings us back to a biblical model that is relevant and addresses the "elephant in the room," which implies that our seminaries are failing to produce successful ministers today. This is a bold pronouncement by the author as he says, "...traditional theological education is founded on an explicit, poisonous doctrine that comes directly from the snake: the choice of the wrong tree... human knowledge."[15] In other words, traditional theological education focuses on the acquiring of knowledge from a textbook, versus the relational experience of knowing God on a personal basis and obeying what He says.

The Word enables us to know Him and the Spirit to experience Him. That is why we are to be Word and Spirit Christians. Word and Spirit Christians are those who are totally committed both to the authority of the Bible and to the indwelling of the Holy Spirit in their lives. The Reformers used a term that is relevant in our day: "*semper reformanda*," a Latin phrase that means, "always reforming." I believe there is a reformation afoot in the church today, especially among younger pastors, to bring both the Spirit and the Word of God to their sheep.

We need the Spirit today. John Piper says:

> The fact that the early Christians prayed so earnestly for signs and wonders is all the more striking when you realize that they, of all generations were in least need of supernatural authentication. This was the generation whose preaching (of Peter, Stephen, Philip, and Paul) was more anointed than the preaching of any generation following. If any preaching was the power of God unto salvation and did not need accompanying signs and wonders, it was this preaching.[16]

Yet the early church needed preaching to validate the gospel message, as we do today.

The power of God was Paul's method of bringing the gospel to people. Paul wrote to the Corinthians of the link between the Word and power:

> My **message** and my **preaching** were not with wise and persuasive **words**, but with a demonstration of the **Spirit's power** (1 Corinthians 2:4 NIV, emphasis added).

> For the kingdom of God does not consist in **words** but in **power** (1 Corinthians 4:20, emphasis added).

We know that in the weapons that we have been given, the sword of the Spirit is the Word. The purpose of the armor of God is to make us strong that we may resist the schemes of the devil. The demonstration of power brings the reality of the kingdom of God to a lost world.

> [10]*Finally, be strong in the Lord and in the strength of his might.* [11]*Put on the whole armor of God, that you may be able to stand against the schemes of the devil* (Ephesians 6:10–11 (ESV).

What is interesting is that the only offensive weapon we have is the Word of God. That is why we need to bury it in our hearts and preach the Word to the lost. The Word of God is the foundation we build upon. If we are not laying a foundation built on the Word of God, then whose foundation are we laying?

> *Take the helmet of salvation and the sword of the **Spirit**, which is the **word of God*** (Ephesians 6:17 NIV, emphasis added).

Paul told the Thessalonians that his gospel was more than just words:

> *because our gospel came to you not simply with **words**, but also with **power**, with the **Holy Spirit** and with deep conviction* (1 Thess 1:5a NIV, emphasis added).

Jesus was devoted to the scriptures and debated with the rabbis using the prophets of the Old Testament. Jesus read the word to the people when He ministered, and so should we, if we are to follow the ministry of Jesus. Luke records this about Jesus: "He **taught** in their synagogues, and everyone praised him. He went to Nazareth, where he had been brought up, and on the Sabbath day he went into the synagogue, as was his custom. And he **stood up to read**" (Lk. 4:15-16 NIV, emphasis added) Did you catch that? Jesus read the scriptures to the people; it was customary for Him. A custom is something that we are in the habit of doing to maintain a tradition, and this was in the context of the local synagogue.[17]

The balance for this next generation is Word and Spirit. David said that he treasured the Word in his heart so that he might not sin against God (Ps. 119:11). We must treasure the Word and embed it in our hearts so that when the day of testing comes we can pull it out to stand on; otherwise we will have a shell without substance. The Word brings substance to our lives, a foundation on which to build.

Building a doctrine on experience only can go all over the place. In our church in the 80s, testimonies became a big thing. One man would get up and tell how he was a drug addict and God delivered him. Then another man would get up and tell a more sensational story of how he was a drug addict and an axe murderer and how God changed his life. The same can be true with experiences; we want to top someone else's experience by being more sensational. If we have a more sensational experience, we think, maybe we can impress those around us as somehow being more intimate with God.

Are experiences normative in the Christian life? Consider Paul's words:

> *¹I must go on boasting. Though there is nothing to be gained by it, I will go on to visions and revelations of the Lord. ²I know a man in Christ who fourteen years ago was caught up to the third heaven—whether in the body or out of the body I do not know, God knows. ³And I know that this man was caught up into paradise—whether in the body or out of the body I do not know, God knows— ⁴and he heard things that cannot be told, which man may not utter. ⁵On behalf of this man I will boast, but on my own behalf I will not boast, except of my weaknesses— ⁶though if I should wish to boast, I would not be a fool, for I would be speaking the truth; but I refrain from it, so that no one may think more of me than he sees in me or hears from me* (2 Corinthians 12:1–6 (ESV).

Obviously, this was not the norm for Paul since he had heard about it fourteen years earlier. God had never let Paul experience that phenomenon. I am not negating or saying that people cannot have this experience, just that it wasn't normative. Why make the sensational normative? Jesus says to seek first the kingdom of God and His righteousness. He does not say, "Seek first experiences," but the kingdom.

When we start to seek experiences, thinking that these are what make us spiritual, we run into the problem of spiritual ethnocentrism; we think we are the best because of these encounters. This can be problematic because we are trying to make the non-normative, normative. Yes, we are seated with Him in heavenly places, but we are to bring His kingdom and His will to earth. He wills that no one perishes and that we love one another. This is the kingdom norm. Love is the new command, the main command, the one thing we are to focus on: love God and love people.

Notes

1 Randy Clark and Mary Healy, *The Spiritual Gifts Handbook; Using Your Gifts to Build the Kingdom.* (Minneapolis: Chosen Books, a division of Baker Publishing Group, 2018).

2 Josh McDowell, *Evidence That Demands a Verdict.* (San Bernardino: Here's Life Publishers, 1979) This book has been revised several times and is a great apologetics book.

3 Norman L. Geisler and Patrick Zukeran. *The Apologetics of Jesus: A Caring Approach to Dealing with Doubters.* (Grand Rapids: Baker Books, 2009). Kindle edition, Location 186.

4 Norman Geisler, *The Apologetics of Jesus*, Kindle Location 203.

5 Alan Hirsch, *The Forgotten Way: Reactivating the Missional Church.* (Grand Rapids: Brazos Press, 2006). Hirsch says that a consumer-driven church is only working in America right now and is not a sustainable model for church growth.

6 Jubilee Resources International, https://jubileeresources.org/?page_id=602

7 Paul Cain and R.T. Kendall, *The Word and The Spirit: Reclaiming Your Covenant with the Holy Spirit and the Word of God.* (East Sussex: Kingsway Publications, 1996). Paul Cain and R.T. Kendall, at the Wembley Conference Center in London in October 1992, took on this subject of being both Word and Spirit.

8 Watchman Nee, *The Gospel of God*, 2-volume set. (Anaheim: Living Stream Ministry, 1990), vol. 1, 154.

9   Gary S. Grieg, *The Kingdom and the Power: Are Healing and the Spiritual Gifts Used by Jesus and the Early Church Meant for the Church Today?* (Ventura: Regal Books, 1993), 179.

10 R.H. Fuller, *The Mission and Achievement of Jesus.* (Chicago: Alec Allenson, 1954), 40.

11 Ruthven, *What's Wrong with Protestant Theology: Traditional Theology vs. Biblical Emphasis*, 42.

12 Ruthven, *What's Wrong with Protestant Theology*, 35.

13 Ruthven, *What's Wrong with Protestant Theology*, 125, 130.

14 Ruthven, *What's Wrong with Protestant Theology*, 252.

15 Ruthven, What's Wrong with Protestant Theology, 274.

16 John Piper, "Signs and Wonders: Then and Now," https://www.desiringgod.org/articles/signs-and-wonders-then-and-now, accessed March 10, 2019.

17 Johannes P. Louw and Eugene Albert Nida. *Greek-English Lexicon of the New Testament: Based on Semantic Domains* (New York: United Bible Societies, 1996), 506.

Chapter Sixteen

Theological Denial

As we begin this final chapter, it is time for me to confess my own theological denial. Theological denial is when one's doctrine overrides clear biblical teaching. For example, in Matthew 7:21–23 Jesus says, [21]"Not everyone who says to me, 'Lord, Lord,' will enter the kingdom of heaven, but the one who does the will of my Father who is in heaven. [22]On that day many will say to me, 'Lord, **Lord, did we not prophesy in your name, and cast out demons in your name, and do many mighty works in your name?'** [23]And then will I declare to them, **'I never knew you; depart from me, you workers of lawlessness'**"(ESV, emphasis added).

How is it possible for people who are prophesying, casting out demons, and doing mighty works for Christ not to be known by Him, but instead called "workers of lawlessness"? "Workers of lawlessness" refers to people who practice sin, because sin is lawless. In the New Testament, we are given a new command, part of the new covenant, and that is to love God and love people. According to the New Testament, we are lawless when we don't love because we are disobeying a command Jesus gave us. Jesus said. "If you love me, you will keep my commandments" (Jn. 14:15 ESV).

[36]*"Teacher, which is the great commandment in the Law?"* [37]*And he said to him, "You shall **love the Lord your God** with all your heart and with all your soul and with all your mind. [38]This is the great and first*

147

commandment. ³⁹*And a second is like it: You shall **love your neighbor as yourself*** (Matthew 22:36–39 ESV, emphasis added).

Being gifted in the charismata doesn't mean necessarily that you are spiritually mature or right with God. At one time, whenever I would exegete 1 Corinthians 12-14, I would always start with 12, then skip over 13 and go straight to 14. Chapter 12 tells us that we need to be informed about spiritual gifts, and chapter 14, that we need to earnestly desire spiritual gifts. So, I would put a heavy emphasis on the gifts but not on love. I thought to myself, "How can Matthew 7 even be relevant? We need to seek the gifts and be passionate about them." The answer to my dilemma resides in 1 Corinthians 13:1–3: ¹"If I speak in the tongues of men and of angels, but have not love, I am a noisy gong or a clanging cymbal. ²And if I have prophetic powers, and understand all mysteries and all knowledge, and if I have all faith, so as to remove mountains, but have not love, I am nothing. ³If I give away all I have, and if I deliver up my body to be burned, but have not love, I gain nothing" (ESV).

If we are to be Word and Spirit people, we need to be people who love and love well, who know God's Word and His Spirit. But it's not enough to know His Word and His Spirit if we don't love others, not only other Christians, but also the people we are trying to reach with the gospel.

A serious question we need to ask ourselves as believers is: When people think of Christians today, what do they think about? David Kinnaman, president of Barna polling, and Gabe Lyons, in their book, *unChristian*¹, present the results of a three-year project in which they polled young, unchurched Americans to find out what they thought about Christianity. Millions of young people, they discovered, see Christians as judgmental, hypocritical, anti-homosexual, too political, insensitive—and boring. Ouch. Yes, in some ways we probably are hypocritical. We have become an oxymoron to our culture because they don't see in us the love of Christ.

An oxymoron, of course, is the joining together of two opposite words to describe something. For example, jumbo shrimp, tiny elephant, pretty ugly or a mean Christian (love is kind). Have we become an oxymoron to our culture today? The tragic irony is that the world as a whole doesn't view us very favorably.

Tim Keller said, "I have a relationship with Christ not because I'm good but precisely because I am not good. He rescued me from myself and the ruin I was causing. But He's changing me. I'm still a mess, but I'm God's mess."[2] Hey, let's face it: we are a mess, and the kingdom can be a mess. Proverbs 14:4 says that where there are no oxen, the stable is clean. This is a euphemism, a lighter way of saying that there is no mess if we don't have oxen in the stable. This is a pastoral challenge for us.

How then is it possible that Christians can be doing the right stuff, yet not going to heaven? The answer to that is the oxymoron of we being "mean" or "unloving" Christians. John tells us why this is so: [7]"Beloved, let us love one another, for love is from God; and everyone who loves is born of God and knows God. [8]**The one who does not love does not know God, for God is love** (1 John 4:7–8, emphasis added). If we don't love we don't know God. There's that Greek word again, *ginosko*. I can't have an intimate relationship with God if I don't love. It's the accusation that Jesus spoke to the Sadducees; they had their doctrine down but they didn't understand the power of God. We can understand the power of God and even have a solid biblical foundation, but we will not be imitators of God unless we learn how to love and to love the unlovely.

John Wesley, at the age of 76, had a young disciple named John Fletcher, who is deservedly called "the systematic theologian of Methodism."[3] On August 5, 1771, Fletcher wrote to Charles (John's brother): "I still want a fountain of power, call it what you please, Baptism of fire, perfect love, sealing, I contend not for the name. In short, I want to be established." Fletcher liked the power and enthusiasm that followed Wesley. As one blogger notes regarding Fletcher's influence on early Methodist beliefs about the Spirit's work in the Christian's life:

> Fletcher didn't exactly teach that Entire Sanctification was "the Baptism in the Holy Spirit" — but he came very close to this.
>
> Particularly relevant is Section 19 of "The Last Check to Antinomianism. A Polemical Essay on the Twin Doctrines of Christian Imperfection and a Death Purgatory." Here he writes:
>
> > Upon the whole, it is, I think, undeniable, from the four first chapters of the Acts, that a peculiar power of the Spirit is bestowed upon believers under the Gospel of Christ; that this power, through faith on our part, can operate the most sudden and surprising change in our souls; and that when our faith shall fully embrace the promise of full sanctification, or of a complete "circumcision of the **heart in the Spirit," the Holy Ghost, who kindled so much love on the day of pentecost, that all the primitive believers loved or seemed to love each other perfectly, will not fail to help us to love one another** without sinful self seeking; and as soon as we do so, 'God dwelleth in us, and his love is perfected in us,' 1 John 4:12; John 14:23.[4]

Wesley and Fletcher believed that the baptism of the Holy Spirit was an empowerment for Christians to love each other perfectly.

William Seymour, the catalyst for the Azusa Street Revival, embraced this thought as well, as Walter J. Hollenweger points out in his essay, "After Twenty Years' Research on Pentecostalism":

> Seymour and his black brothers suffered bitterly. During Seymour's adult lifetime 3436 black persons were known to have been lynched, averaging two a week. Innumerable brutalities took place around him, many of them instigated by Christians. In spite of constant humiliation he developed a spirituality that in 1906 led to a revival in Los Angeles that most Pentecostal historians believe to be the cradle of pentecostalism. The roots of Seymour's spirituality lay in his past. He affirmed his black heritage by introducing Negro spirituals and Negro music into his liturgy at a time when this music was considered inferior

and unfit for Christian worship. At the same time he steadfastly lived out his understanding of pentecost. **For him pentecost meant more than speaking in tongues. It meant to love in the face of hate, to overcome the hatred with a whole nation by demonstrating that pentecost is something very different from the success-oriented American way of life.**[5]

I am a pro-tongues person, as I said in the beginning; I have been speaking in tongues since I was 16. I have encouraged and prayed for thousands to receive the gift of tongues. If you don't speak in tongues, ask Jesus and He will give you the gift. What I am saying is that for Seymour the baptism of the Holy Spirit was more than this. Seymour was an "initial evidence" person, that is, that speaking in tongues is the evidence that you are baptized in the Holy Spirit.[6] In 1915, he published a guidebook for the mission and churches that grew from it: *The Doctrines and Discipline of the Azusa Street Apostolic Faith Mission, Los Angeles, California.* It was the only book he ever wrote, but it is still available today in reprints.[7] A couple of quotes from the book show clearly what Seymour believed regarding Spirit baptism:
First:

The baptism in the Holy Ghost and fire means to be flooded with the love of God and power for service, and a love for the truth as it is in God's word. So when we receive it we have the same signs to follow as the disciples received on the day of Pentecost. For the Holy Spirit gives us a sound mind, faith, love and power (2 Tim. 1:7). This is the standard Jesus gave to the church (emphasis added).

And:

I can say, through the power of the Spirit, that wherever God can get a people that will come together in one accord and one mind in the Word of God, the baptism of the Holy Ghost will fall upon them, like as at Cornelius' house (Acts 10:45,46). It means, to be in one accord, as the word says in Acts 2:42,47. [8]

I want to make it very clear here that I am not negating speaking in tongues, prophesying, or the working of miracles. This is one of those "either/or" scenarios that we talked about earlier. People want to polarize into opposite camps and we need to bring the camps together so that we operate in the gifts and love well. For us, this is a "both/and" situation.

We need to operate in the gifts and learn to love the unlovely if we don't want to be noisy gongs or clanging cymbals, in Paul's words. For Seymour, the baptism of the Holy Spirit was much more than speaking in tongues: "We are not seeking for tongues, but we are seeking the baptism with the Holy Ghost and fire. And when we receive it we shall be so filled with the Holy Ghost, that He Himself will speak in the power of the Spirit."[9] Acts 1:8 says that we will receive power from the Holy Spirit to be a witness. We desire tongues so we will be built up, increase our effectiveness in prayer, and be prepared for spiritual warfare. Tongues are needed today as much as they were in Paul's day. Tongues equip us to carry out the work of the ministry. If you don't speak in tongues, ask God, and He will give this gift to you.

Think about what an impact the Pentecostal movement has had on the world today.[10] What would it look like today if tongues was not the primary focus of early Pentecostalism and empowerment of love and tongues was? Would racial tensions be as strong today? Would political tensions be as strong today? Would church unity be any better if an empowerment of love was the focus? Seymour overcame racial prejudice by the power of the Holy Spirit, which enabled him to love. One Los Angeles Times article written at the time said of the Azusa Street revival that, "the color line was washed away in the blood". Again, remember that these events took place before the Civil Rights Movement. In the midst of racial segregation, Seymour chose to love.[11]

When there is a move of God, people often seek for the manifestation that is happening instead of the effect. For example, the same can be said about the Toronto Blessing and seeking the experience over the intent of the outpouring.

In 1994, I was in Southern California and was part of the Toronto outpouring at our local church. For two years we had meetings every night. We witnessed tremendous miracles almost daily. However, at our church, it ended within two years. The reason it ended was because for us, it became all about getting blasted in the Holy Spirit. "Getting blasted" is a phrase coined in the Toronto Blessing that generally means experiencing the power of the Holy Spirit in a dramatic way. Oftentimes, getting blasted is associated with falling to the ground, feeling drunk in the Spirit, or some other effect of the Holy Spirit. People at our church started to seek the effect rather than the effect-Giver. Whereas with the Azusa Street revival it became about speaking in tongues, for us it became about getting blasted in the Holy Spirit. Today, more than 20 years later, people still talk about the Toronto Blessing, usually either in terms of amazement or in a derogatory manner as some type of "strange fire."[12]

What was the effect of the Toronto Blessing? Margret Paloma, a sociologist, discusses the effects of this outpouring in her book, *Main Street Mystics*. Some have tried to demonize the Toronto Blessing by labeling it as a heretical movement. Paloma's research reported its positive effects:

> Most respondents have experienced several different manifestations, with only 1 percent reporting that they have never had any. These ranged from glossolalia (tongues), to wild shaking, jerking and rolling, to appearing "drunk", to quietly falling to the floor ("carpet time"). Judging from the reported effects, it would appear that indeed the Spirit of God is at work.
>
> The responses to the survey reflect well the impressions that continue to be reinforced through the verbal testimonies given regularly at services. The manifestations, while not necessary for the "change

of heart" that is the focus of the testimonies, often do accompany significant changes in those who have visited TACF. Seventy percent (70%) of the respondents noted that friends and family have commented on such changes. (Only 10% said that they could see no change in their lives that they would attribute to their visit to TACF.) The effects may be described as increases in personal spiritual refreshment, holiness and healing, and evangelism and social outreach. Although approximately 50 percent of the respondents reported coming to TACF while "spiritually dry," most left with a deeper sense of God's love for them. Ninety-one percent (91%) said they had a greater sense of the Father's love and 89 percent reported being more in love with Jesus than ever before as a result of their time at TACF. This greater awareness was often coupled with a new sense of sinfulness, with over half (54%) reporting they had experienced some form of deliverance from the hold of the devil on their lives. While only 1 percent of the respondents reported giving their lives to the Lord for the first time.

The fresh experience of God's love and forgiveness often brought with it personal healing, the most common of which was an "inner healing" (reported by 78 percent of the respondents). Twenty-two percent (22%) claimed they received some physical healing, and six percent (6%) acknowledged a healing from a clinically diagnosed mental health problem. The benefits of the Blessing appear to extend to the whole person--touching the body, the mind, and the spirit.

People also reported changes in relationships. Eighty-eight percent (88%) of those who were married claimed to be more in love with their spouses than ever before. Thirty-seven percent (37%) said they had become more involved in works of mercy, like feeding the hungry or visiting those in prisons. They were also more likely (83%) to share their Christian faith with others than ever before. Perhaps reflecting these personal changes, 71 percent reported that the "Toronto Blessing" had a positive impact on their churches, with only 10 percent saying that the response of their church community to the Blessing was a "negative" one.[13]

The effects of the outpouring in Toronto were more than just tongues, more than just getting blasted, and more than just falling to the ground. Jesus said, ¹⁶"You will know them by their fruits. Grapes are not gathered from thorn bushes nor figs from thistles, are they? ¹⁷"So every good tree bears good fruit, but the bad tree bears bad fruit" (Mt. 7:16-17). The fruit of this outpouring had tremendous impact, yet so many got caught up in the manner that it happened.

Our local church turned this outpouring into seeking an effect, and so we missed what God was doing. It became about us when it was never meant to be about us. It was meant to reach the lost and hurting of this world. According to Paloma's research, God was healing people both physically and emotionally. He was changing people's lives, empowering people, and setting people on fire.

If we are going to change the world, we need to be changed first, empowered by God to love radically, and then go and do the stuff that Jesus did. There is a shift in our world today. People are not hungry for hypocritical religion; they are hungry for a loving God who can change their lives. They are desperate, but the question is, are we desperate to follow Him, to take risks for Him, and to get out of our comfort zones of the consumer-driven church? "And he said to all, 'If anyone would come after me, let him deny himself and take up his cross daily and follow me'" Lk. 9:23 (ESV).

In 1860, Blondine, a famous tightrope walker, strung a 1,000-foot cable 160 feet above the roaring waters of Niagara Falls. Large crowds gathered on both sides of the falls to watch while he performed his fearless acts of daring. Having made a number of trips back and forth over the wire, he came down to his audience and asked them, "Do you believe I can walk across the wire one more time?" A resounding cheer of affirmation erupted from the crowd. Again, the daredevil queried the people: "Do you believe I could cross the wire while carrying a man on my back?" Again, the crowd roared their conformation. To this, the performer asked, "Which one of you will be first?" The air went silent as everyone looked at the ground, avoiding his inquiring gaze. It is easy for us to believe in something that demands little from us.

The faith required to accept the gospel is one that embraces our Lord with a wholehearted trust that Christ can do what He claims.[14]

> You see; with mental assent you believe something in your head, you agree, approve and confirm it is right, proper and righteous. It carries your unwavering endorsement. You may not talk about it, but it bears your seal of approval....Only by acting (signing or commiting) do you actually express what you believe. You see why it is easy to approve of something in your mind, vicariously, as though you were a participant, but not actually do it yourself? It is self-deceiving to claim to believe without corresponding action. That's mental assent and it can only end in failure.[15]

In a sermon entitled, "The Almost Christian," based on King Agrippa's encounter with the apostle Paul, John Wesley described an "almost Christian" as one who is willing to go "only thus far, almost persuaded to be a Christian." He gave three characteristics of an "almost Christian":

1. "Heathen honesty"; what we would call human decency or basic goodness.
2. A "form of religion"; religious practice, doing good, avoiding evil—all the outward appearances of a Christian, except in worship, displaying inattention, listlessness, indifference, even sleeping.
3. Sincerity—A desire to serve God, to do his will.

An almost Christian wavers between serving God and serving the world.

It is time for us to get off the pews and go out into our world. It is time for pastors not to fear what people in their congregations think. It is time to be the church that God dreams about, one that embraces the old and makes it new.

By embracing the old, we are not seeking a new program; the program was set in the Book of Acts. We need to bring the power of God to a lost generation and let them know that there is hope only in Jesus. This is when the old becomes new, and when the old becomes the resurrected norm for turning the world upside down, we need the Book of Acts today. If we do this, I believe that we will be the church that turns the world upside down in a great end times revival. I would encourage you to implement the techniques that are in this book. If you do, you will see miracles and you will start to hear God's voice. I have trained so many people to do this. The hard part is stepping out in faith. Faith, as John Wimber said, is spelled R-I-S-K. It really is like the old sports show, ABC's Wide World of Sports, which opened each program with the slogan, "The thrill of victory and the agony of defeat." There will be times when you see amazing things happen for Jesus, and other times when you don't see anything happen. The key here is not to find your identify in your gift, but in the Gift-Giver. The walk that we have in Jesus is an adventure. I invite you to join Him and help change the world. If we do, we will get the reputation that is recorded in Acts 17:6b (ESV): "These men who have turned the world upside down have come here also."[16]

Notes

1   David Kinnaman and Gabe Lyons, *unChristian: What a New Generation Really Thinks about Christianity...and Why It Matters.* (Grand Rapids: Baker Publishing House. 2012)

2   Tim Keller, interviewed by Ed Stetzer, researcher, blogger, and host of Inside Lifeway, posted April 24, 2008, lifeway.edgeboss.net/download/lifeway/corp/IL_Evangelism_and_Keller.mp3.

3   John A. Knight, "John Fletcher's Influence on the Development of Wesleyan Theology in America," *Wesleyan Theological Journal, Spring 1978,* 17.

4   Craig L. Adams, "Spirit Baptism: Wesleyanism & Pentecostalism," https://craigladams.com/blog/spirit-baptism-wesleyanism-pentecostalism/, accessed March 18, 2019.

5   Walter J. Hollenweger, "After Twenty Years' Research on Pentecostalism," quoted in Luke Garaty, "William Seymour's 'love in the face of hate,'" (emphasis in original), http://thinktheology.org/2014/10/08/william-seymours-love-face-hate/, accessed March 18, 2019.

6   Initial evidence is the theology of classic Pentecostal denominations that believes that the speaking of lounges is the evidence that you are baptized in the Holy Spirit. William Parham, William Seymour's mentor, is the one who help to initiate this doctrine.

7   William J. Seymour, *The Doctrines and Discipline of the Azusa Street Apostolic Faith Mission of Los Angeles. The Complete Azusa Street Library* (Joplin: Christian Life Books, 2000).

8   William J. Seymour, *The Doctrines*.

9   Reve' M. Pete, *William Seymour's Teaching at Azusa Street Mission: The Impact of Holiness Preaching as Taught by John Wesley and the Outpouring of the Holy Ghost on Racism.* This is out of Dr. Pete's dissertation at Bethany Divinity College and Seminary at Albany Georgia. (Chapter 10, "William Seymour's Teaching at the Azusa Street Mission).

10 Keener, *Miracles,* vol.1&2.

11 Frank Barttleman, *How Pentecost Came to Los Angeles.* (Springfield: Gospel Publishing House). Barttleman, notes that the racial lines were completely washed away at the revival.

12 John MacArthur, *Strange Fire: The Danger of Offending the Holy Spirit with Counterfeit Worship.* (Nashville: Thomas Nelson Publishers, 2013). In his book MacArthur lambastes the Toronto Blessing, claiming it was not of God. Many rebuttal books have been written. My favorite is Robert Graves, *Strangers to Fire: When Tradition Trumps Scripture.* (Westbrook: The Foundations for Pentecostal Scholarship, 2014). It is a collection of 35 essays by noted scholars that refute MacArthur's position.

13 Margret Paloma, *Main Street Mystics: The Toronto Blessing and Reviving Pentecostalism.* (Walnut Creek: Altimira Press, 2003).

14 Mark A. Holmes, *Ephesians: A Bible Commentary in the Wesleyan Tradition.* (Indianapolis: Wesleyan Publishing House, 1997), 50.

15 Tim Greenwood, "Mental Assent—The Enemy of Faith," Dec. 28, 2007, https://tgm.org/mental-assent-the-enemy-of-faith/, accessed March 18, 2019.

16 Ron Smith, *Private Prayer, Public Power* (Lakeside: www.ronsmithbooks.com 2004).

Ron says that the Apostle Paul gives 7 reasons why he prayed privately in tongues.
1. Spiritual Warfare
2. Personal Edification
3. Prayer with His Spirit
4. Uttering Mysteries to God
5. Prayers of Blessing
6. Prayers of Thanksgiving
7. Intercession

About the Author

Dr. Nick Gough has been in ministry for over 35 years. He is a frequent speaker for YWAM and the Foursquare denomination. He is an adjunct professor for Global Awakening Theological Seminary in Shawnee, Oklahoma. Nick pastors a local church in Great Falls, Montana, has planted numerous churches, and is a divisional supervisor for the Foursquare International Church. Dr. Nick has a passion to see the invisible kingdom of God touch a generation for Jesus. He has been married for 30 years and has five beautiful daughters.

eGenco

Generation Culture Transformation
Specializing in publishing for generation culture change

Visit us Online at:
www.egen.co

Write to: eGenco
824 Tallow Hill Road
Chambersburg, PA 17202, USA
Phone: 717-461-3436
Email: info@egen.com

facebook.com/egenbooks
youtube.com/egenpub
egen.co/blog
pinterest.com/eGenDMP
twitter.com/egen_co
instagram.com/egen.co